~~worry~~

~~cry~~

~~argue~~

~~fight~~

pray first

the transformative power
of a life built on prayer

BIBLE STUDY GUIDE | SIX SESSIONS

CHRIS HODGES

HarperChristian
Resources

Pray First Bible Study Guide
© 2023 by Chris Hodges

Requests for information should be addressed to:
HarperChristian Resources, 3900 Sparks Dr. SE, Grand Rapids, Michigan 49546

ISBN 978-0-310-15895-0 (softcover)
ISBN 978-0-310-15896-7 (ebook)

CONTENTS

A Note from Chris V

How to Use This Guide vii

SESSION 1: The Five P's of Prayer

Group Section 1

Personal Study 13

    Day 1: Pray First 14
    Day 2: Pray God's Word 17
    Day 3: Cultivate a Lifestyle of Prayer 20
    Day 4: Take Inventory 22
    Day 5: Take Action 26

SESSION 2: The Lord's Prayer

Group Section 29

Personal Study 41

    Day 1: Pray First 42
    Day 2: Pray God's Word 45
    Day 3: Cultivate a Lifestyle of Prayer 48
    Day 4: Take Inventory 50
    Day 5: Take Action 52

SESSION 3: The Prayer of Jabez

Group Section 55

Personal Study 65

    Day 1: Pray First 66
    Day 2: Pray God's Word 69
    Day 3: Cultivate a Lifestyle of Prayer 72
    Day 4: Take Inventory 74
    Day 5: Take Action 76

SESSION 4: Praying the Names of God

Group Section 79

Personal Study 91

 Day 1: Pray First 92
 Day 2: Pray God's Word 95
 Day 3: Cultivate a Lifestyle of Prayer 98
 Day 4: Take Inventory 100
 Day 5: Take Action 102

SESSION 5: My Prayer for You

Group Section 105

Personal Study 117

 Day 1: Pray First 118
 Day 2: Pray God's Word 121
 Day 3: Cultivate a Lifestyle of Prayer 124
 Day 4: Take Inventory 126
 Day 5: Take Action 128

SESSION 6: Prayer and Fasting

Group Section 131

Personal Study 141

 Day 1: Pray First 142
 Day 2: Pray God's Word 144
 Day 3: Cultivate a Lifestyle of Prayer 147
 Day 4: Take Inventory 149
 Day 5: Take Action 150

Leader's Guide 153

Endnotes 159

A NOTE FROM CHRIS

Prayer is the lifeblood of the Christian faith. But it's also one of the most misunder-stood parts of following Jesus. You may view prayer as a natural ability—like athletic strength, musical talent, or a great sense of humor—and assume you don't have what it takes. Or perhaps you consider prayer an acquired skill that relies on prac-tice. So you put in your time diligently but don't particularly enjoy prayer or pray spontaneously. You might even view prayer as a last resort, a kind of supernatural SOS when you need help and don't know what to do.

Instead of an awkward obligation, item to check off your schedule, or your last re-sort, prayer can become your first response. Fundamentally, prayer is about con-necting with God and confronting the enemy. Prayer keeps your faith alive, your hope in Christ strong, and your relationship with God healthy. Prayer helps you avoid temptation and resist the snares set by the devil. The importance of prayer in sustaining your faith cannot be overestimated.

The Bible repeatedly indicates that prayer is not optional—it's essential to knowing God. The Lord wants us to view prayer as the vibrant foundation of our relationship with him. We're told to "pray continually" (1 Thessalonians 5:17) and to be "faithful in prayer" (Romans 12:12), not just sporadically, or occasionally, when we're in church or when we feel like it.

While praying continually may sound challenging or even impossible, connecting with God in the midst of every part of your day draws you closer to him. Prayer anchors you in truth and helps you maintain an eternal perspective, freeing you from circumstantial worries and temporary trials. "Do not be anxious about any-thing," God's Word says, "but in every situation, by prayer and petition, with thanks-giving, present your requests to God" (Philippians 4:6).

By weaving prayer into the fabric of your daily life, you make it the priority God intended and prayer becomes central to your lifestyle. As you realize how talking and listening to God draw you closer to him, you enjoy the intimacy you've longed to experience. You experience the peace that passes all human understanding (see Philippians 4:7) and take shelter in the unconditional love of your heavenly Father (see Romans 8:38–39).

The key to allowing prayer to permeate your life is simply to put it first. When the Bible instructs you to pray continually, the emphasis is not on perpetual repetition but on importance and consistency. God wants you to *pray first* in all situations. He wants you to thank him, ask him, trust him, seek him, listen to him, and enjoy all the blessings that he bestows.

When you pray first, you keep in constant contact with Almighty God, the Creator of heaven and earth, who also happens to be your Abba Father, your lavishly loving Papa. When you pray first, you have access to God the Father through Jesus the Son, who has paid the price for your sin and now intercedes on your behalf without ceasing. When you pray first, the Holy Spirit sticks with you more closely than any friend and helps you pray when you don't even know how to express yourself with words. When you pray first, your faith matures and you bear the spiritual fruit God that has planted in you.

Regardless of your past experiences with prayer, how often or little you pray, or whatever feelings you may have, it's time to discover the depth of joy, peace, and purpose that only comes when you *pray first*.

— Chris Hodges

HOW TO USE THIS GUIDE

What would it look like if you brought God into every area of your life each day? This is the goal of the *Pray First* study—to help you experience the abundance of the Christian life by showing you how to interact with God on a daily and consistent basis.

To this end, in session 1 you will begin by exploring the fundamentals of prayer—the *priority, place, plan, power,* and *Persons* of prayer. In sessions 2–5, you will examine models of prayer drawn from Scripture, including the Lord's Prayer, the Prayer of Jabez, and several others for protection, provision, and power in overcoming the enemy. In the final session, you will look at the often-misunderstood pairing of fasting with prayer.

Before you begin, note there are a few ways you can go through this material. You can experience this study with others in a group (such as a Bible study, Sunday school class, or any other small-group gathering), or you may choose to go through the content on your own. Either way, know that the videos for each session are available for you to view at any time by following the instructions provided on the inside cover of this study guide.

GROUP STUDY

Each session in this guide is divided into two parts: (1) a group study section, and (2) a personal study section. The group section provides a framework on how to open your time together, get the most out of the video content, and discuss the key ideas together that were presented in the teaching. Each session includes the following:

- **Welcome:** A short note about the topic of the session for you to read on your own before you meet as a group.
- **Connect:** A few icebreaker questions to get you and your group members thinking about the topic and interacting with each other.
- **Watch:** An outline of the key points covered in each video teaching to help you follow along, stay engaged, and take notes.
- **Discuss:** Questions to help your group reflect on the teaching material presented and apply it to your lives. In each session, you will be given four suggested questions and four additional questions to use as time allows.
- **Respond:** A short personal exercise to help reinforce the key ideas.
- **Pray:** A place for you to record prayer requests and praises for the week.

If you are doing this study in a group, make sure you have your own copy of the study guide so you can write down your thoughts, responses, and reflections—and so you have access to the videos via streaming. You will also want to have a copy of the *Pray First* book, as reading it alongside the curriculum will provide you with deeper insights. (See the notes at the beginning of each group session and personal study section on which chapters of the book you should read before the next group session.)

Finally, keep these points in mind:

- **Facilitation:** If you are doing this study in a group, you will want to appoint someone to serve as a facilitator. This person will be responsible for starting the video and keeping track of time during discussions and activities. If *you* have been chosen for this role, there are some resources in the back of this guide that can help you lead your group through the study.

- **Faithfulness:** Your group is a place where tremendous growth can happen as you reflect on the Bible, ask questions, and learn what God is doing in other people's lives. For this reason, be fully committed and attend each session so you can build trust and rapport with the other members.

- **Friendship:** The goal of any small group is to serve as a place where people can share, learn about God, and build friendships. So seek to make your group a "safe place." Be honest about your thoughts and feelings, but also listen carefully to everyone else's thoughts, feelings, and opinions. Keep anything personal that your group members share in confidence so that you can create a community where people can heal, be challenged, and grow spiritually.

If you are going through this study on your own, read the opening Welcome section and reflect on the questions in the Connect section. Watch the video and use the prompts provided to take notes. Finally, personalize the questions and exercises in the Discuss and Respond sections. Close by recording any requests you want to pray about during the week.

PERSONAL STUDY

The personal study is for you to work through on your own during the week. Each exercise is designed to help you explore the key ideas you uncovered during your group time and delve into passages of Scripture that will help you apply those principles to your life. Go at your own pace, doing a little each day—or tackle the material all at once. Remember to spend a few moments in silence to listen to whatever God might be saying to you.

Here is a general outline of each week's study:

- **Day 1 (Pray First):** You will refamiliarize yourself with the content presented during your group time and start to consider how to apply it to your life.

- **Day 2 (Pray God's Word):** You will read a passage on a key topic covered during your group time and engage in a few questions and exercises designed to help you apply the truths of that passage to your situation.

- **Day 3 (Cultivate a Lifestyle of Prayer):** You will read a passage from *Pray First* and start to develop a plan for making prayer a lifestyle.

- **Day 4 (Take Inventory):** You will be given a chance to take inventory on your life and really assess how to implement these strategies on prayer.

- **Day 5 (Take Action):** You will get even more specific on actions that you will take to develop your prayer life and intimacy with God. You will also read the chapters in *Pray First* that correspond to the next session.

Note that if you are doing this study as part of a group, and you are unable to finish (or even start) these personal studies for the week, you should still attend the group time. Be assured that you are still wanted and welcome even if you don't have your "homework" done. The group studies and personal studies are intended to help you hear what God wants you to hear and understand how to apply what he is saying to your life. So . . . as you go through this study, be listening for him to speak to you as you learn how to make prayer a greater priority in your life.

schedule

WEEK 1

BEFORE GROUP MEETING	Read the Introduction and chapters 1–5 in *Pray First* Read the Welcome section (page 2)
GROUP MEETING	Discuss the Connect questions Watch the video teaching for session 1 Discuss the questions that follow as a group Do the closing exercise and pray (pages 2–12)
PERSONAL STUDY – DAY 1	Complete the daily study (pages 14–16)
PERSONAL STUDY – DAY 2	Complete the daily study (pages 17–19)
PERSONAL STUDY – DAY 3	Complete the daily study (pages 20–21)
PERSONAL STUDY – DAY 4	Complete the daily study (pages 22–25)
PERSONAL STUDY – DAY 5 (BEFORE WEEK 2 GROUP MEETING)	Read chapter 6 in *Pray First* Complete any unfinished personal studies (pages 26–27)

the five p's of prayer

Prayer is easier than you think and more important than you realize.

CHRIS HODGES

WELCOME | READ ON YOUR OWN

"Well, there's nothing left to do but pray."

Have you ever heard someone make this statement? Or even said those words yourself? Perhaps the comment reflected a medical situation in which nothing seemed to be helping. It could have been uttered in response to a relationship with a loved one struggling with addiction. You might have found yourself thinking that prayer was your last resort when you lost your job, discovered a friend's betrayal, or mourned the unexpected death of someone you loved.

Perhaps you want to pray more, but you feel intimidated, uncertain, and sometimes embarrassed about how to talk to God. Based on past experiences, false assumptions, or faulty misperceptions, prayer may be relegated to church services, grace at mealtimes, and desperate moments in crisis. But what if prayer could be a natural, inherent part of your daily rhythms? What if prayer could connect you to God in ways you've never experienced?

While prayer can be a struggle, it's also the lifeblood of the Christian faith and more than worth reconsidering and practicing anew. You might be surprised how learning and implementing some simple fundamentals can change the way you consider prayer and, more importantly, incorporate it into your everyday life.

Yes, sometimes prayer is the *only* thing we can do, but it is always the *best* thing we can do. Rather than your last resort, it's time to make prayer your first response!

CONNECT | 15 MINUTES

If you or any of your group members don't know each other, take a few minutes to introduce yourselves. Then, to get things started, discuss one of the following questions:

- What immediately comes to mind when you think of prayer? Why?

  — or —

- What did you learn about prayer, for better or worse, when you were growing up?

James 5:16

WATCH | 20 MINUTES

Now it's time to watch the video for this session, which you can access by playing the DVD or through streaming (see the instructions provided on the inside front cover). As you watch, use the following outline to record any thoughts or concepts that stand out to you.

I. The **priority** of prayer

   A. God will listen to our prayers and answer our prayers at any time throughout the day, but there's something special about giving prayer a place—a priority—in our lives.

   B. There is something special about starting the day by spending a few minutes with God.

   C. Set aside a quiet time with God in the morning—a morning time of prayer—by putting God on your calendar. Actually give God a space in your schedule at the beginning of the day.

II. The **place** of prayer

    A. Find a specific place where you will pray. It's not that you can't pray in other places, or that you will always pray in the same location, but find a primary place where you will pray.

    B. In Mark 1:35, we read that Jesus would retreat to a special *place* to pray. Early in the morning, while it was still dark, he went off to a solitary place to pray.

    C. If Jesus had a special place to pray, you should have a special place as well. So, your assignment on this point is to find that special place where you will pray.

III. The **plan** of prayer

    A. Prayer is simply having a conversation with God, but it's important to go into that conversation with a plan. Think about who and what you want to bring to God in prayer.

B. When the disciples saw Jesus praying, they asked him to teach them how to pray in the way that he prayed. Jesus responded with a plan—what today we call the Lord's Prayer.

C. Always have a plan so you never get to the place where you don't know what to say in prayer.

IV. The **power** of prayer

A. Prayer is a conversation with God, but there is also a spiritual element to prayer. When we pray, we are confronting the enemy and dealing in the heavenlies.

B. In Acts 4:29, we read the prayer that the disciples Peter and John prayed after being released from prison. They asked for God to enable them to speak his word with boldness.

C. We need to likewise pray bold prayers, believing that he will perform mighty works on our behalf. Effective prayers have an energy to them.

V. The **Person** of prayer

    A. Prayer is not about prayer. Prayer is about the Person to whom the prayers are directed. You are spending time with the Father, the Son, and the Holy Spirit.

    B. In 2 Corinthians 13:14, Paul mentions all three members of the Godhead.

        1. Jesus is the mediator. He is the one delivering our prayers to God. He is the one who made it possible through the cross.

        2. God is the Father who loves his children. We don't come crawling before him in prayer but sit as his feet like someone we love and respect.

3. **The Holy Spirit is the friend.** He is always present and with us every moment of our lives.

C. These are the fundamentals of prayer. If you will begin to apply these fundamentals in your life, prayer is going to work and you are going to find it so much more enjoyable.

DISCUSS | 35 MINUTES

Discuss what you just watched by answering the following questions as time allows.

I. The first fundamental of making prayer work in your life is to make it a *priority*. What would you have to rearrange in your schedule to make prayer a priority?

2. The second fundamental of making prayer work in your life is to have a *place* for prayer. What place would be most conducive for prayer to work for you?

3. The third fundamental of making prayer work in your life is to have a *plan*. What are some steps that you can take this week to create a plan for your prayer time?

4. The fourth fundamental of making prayer work in your life is to recognize the *power* of prayer. What hurdles will you have to overcome to make prayer a powerful experience?

5. The fifth fundamental of making prayer work in your life is to recognize the *Persons* of prayer. Which of the three *Persons* of the Godhead—Father, Son, and Holy Spirit—do you tend to address when you pray? Which Person do you tend to overlook when you pray?

6. Which of the three Persons of the Godhead seems the most accessible to you? Explain your response.

7. Which of the five *P*'s of prayer reflects aspects of prayer that you haven't considered before? Which one stands out to you as requiring more emphasis in your own prayer life?

8. What is the Holy Spirit saying to you about these fundamentals of prayer? Which of the five *P*'s do you feel drawn to be more deliberate in practicing when you pray?

RESPOND | 10 MINUTES

As mentioned in the video, the members of the early church entered into prayer expecting God to show up and do mighty things on their behalf. But they also prayed to receive boldness and power from God so that they could continue to share the message of Christ. Read the following passage about one of these prayers on your own and then answer the questions that follow.

> [1] The priests and the captain of the temple guard and the Sadducees came up to Peter and John while they were speaking to the people. [2] They were greatly disturbed because the apostles were teaching the people, proclaiming in Jesus the resurrection of the dead. [3] They seized Peter and John and, because it was evening, they put them in jail until the next day. . . .
>
> [23] On their release, Peter and John went back to their own people and reported all that the chief priests and the elders had said to them. [24] When they heard this, they raised their voices together in prayer to God. "Sovereign Lord," they said, "you made the heavens and the earth and the sea, and everything in them. . . .
>
> [29] "Now, Lord, consider their threats and enable your servants to speak your word with great boldness. [30] Stretch out your hand to heal and perform signs and wonders through the name of your holy servant Jesus."
>
> [31] After they prayed, the place where they were meeting was shaken. And they were all filled with the Holy Spirit and spoke the word of God boldly.
>
> **Acts 4:1–3, 23–24, 29–31**

What stands out to you about the way the early believers regarded prayer?

How similar or different is that to the way modern believers approach prayer?

What word or phrase stands out in this passage? Why does it strike a chord?

PRAY | 10 MINUTES

Conclude your time by actually praying for one another. Go around the room and share any requests that you would like the group to pray about, and then pray for those requests together, either silently or out loud. Thank God for bringing you all together to focus on prayer so that you can grow stronger in your relationship with the Lord and with one another. Make sure you include all three Persons of God during your prayer time as you begin practicing what you've learned in this first session. Finally, use the space below to take notes on the requests that are mentioned so you can continue to pray about them in the week ahead.

Name   Request

personal
STUDY

You are on a journey toward a better understanding of how to put prayer first in your life. A key part of that growth, regardless of where you are spiritually, involves studying Scripture. This is the goal of these personal studies—to help you explore what the Bible has to say and how to apply God's Word to your life. As you work through each of these exercises, be sure to write down your responses to the questions, as you will be given a few minutes to share your insights at the start of the next session if you are doing this study with others. If you are reading *Pray First* alongside this study, first read the Introduction and chapters 1–5 of the book.

— DAY 1 —
PRAY FIRST

When prioritizing prayer in your life, you may be tempted to assume that God prefers quality over quantity. But the Bible reveals that God wants *both* our full attention and engaged heart in the midst of everything we do every day. Praying just to check an item off a to-do list misses the point of prayer and results in your losing an opportunity to connect to your heavenly Father.

During Jesus' time on earth, he demonstrated both quality and quantity in his prayer life. He knew the importance of getting away from the clamor of the crowds to connect with his Father: "Very early in the morning, while it was still dark, Jesus got up, left the house and went off to a solitary place, where he prayed" (Mark 1:35). This pattern of praying continued throughout his human life (see Matthew 14:23, Luke 9:18, Luke 22:39–41). Looking in the Gospels, you will find at least three dozen other occasions when Jesus prayed.

Based on Jesus' example, for prayer to be a priority in your life, you must also cultivate a lifestyle of prayer, engaging deliberately and purposefully on a daily basis. As daunting as it might sound to "pray continually" (1 Thessalonians 5:17), you can still practice praying as much as you can while doing everything else in your day. Prayer is about living in connection to God and, through that connection, living out his purpose for your life. This is why it's important for you to talk to God *before* you act, *before* you decide, *before* you're tempted, *before* you speak, *before* you risk. In other words . . . to *pray first*!

With this goal in mind, read the following passage and answer the questions below.

³ Trust in the Lord and do good;
    dwell in the land and enjoy safe pasture.
⁴ Take delight in the Lord,
    and he will give you the desires of your heart.

⁵ Commit your way to the Lord;
    trust in him and he will do this:
⁶ He will make your righteous reward shine like the dawn,
    your vindication like the noonday sun.

> [7] Be still before the LORD
>   and wait patiently for him;
> do not fret when people succeed in their ways,
>   when they carry out their wicked schemes. . . .
>
> [23] The LORD makes firm the steps
>   of the one who delights in him;
> [24] though he may stumble, he will not fall,
>   for the LORD upholds him with his hand.
>
> **Psalm 37:3–7, 23–24**

I. On a scale of 1 to 10, with 1 being lowest and 10 being highest, what score reflects prayer as a priority in your life right now?

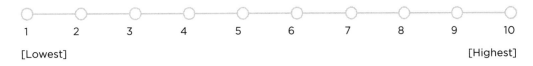

1   2   3   4   5   6   7   8   9   10

[Lowest]   [Highest]

What other priorities are interfering with making prayer a major priority?

2. When you think of people in the Bible known for praying, who comes to mind? Why does that person stand out to you?

3. What strikes you about the way Jesus incorporated prayer throughout his earthly life? What quality of his would you like to emulate in your own prayer life?

4. Considering the psalm above, would you describe a stronger prayer life as a "desire of your heart" (verse 4)? What obstacles are hindering the fulfillment of this desire?

5. How often are you presently able to "be still before the Lᴏʀᴅ and wait patiently for him" (verse 7)? How can this posture help you prioritize prayer?

6. When was the last time you prayed before making a decision or taking action? What would be required for you to regularly pray first rather than after the fact?

— DAY 2 —
PRAY GOD'S WORD

Reconsidering what you know about prayer and the ways to incorporate it into your life can reinvigorate your faith in amazing ways. This is why it's important to develop prayer routines and habits that help you focus on God as you talk to him. Having a plan for your prayer times can help ensure that you won't wander, daydream, or shift into autopilot as you pray.

Praying verses and passages from God's Word is one of the best ways to help you focus. Plans built around Scripture immerse your mind and heart in truth as you connect with God and confront the enemy. For this reason, through these personal studies, you will be encouraged to pray a passage from the Bible relevant to that session's big ideas. But if you feel led to pray a different verse or passage, don't hesitate to follow that prompting of the Holy Spirit.

Almost immediately after Jesus taught his disciples how to pray (see Luke 11:1–4), he explained the importance of desire and persistence when it comes to seeking God and his will. Read through Christ's descriptive instruction, underlining or circling any words or phrases that jump out to you, and then answer the questions that follow.

> [5] Then Jesus said to them, "Suppose you have a friend, and you go to him at midnight and say, 'Friend, lend me three loaves of bread; [6] a friend of mine on a journey has come to me, and I have no food to offer him.' [7] And suppose the one inside answers, 'Don't bother me. The door is already locked, and my children and I are in bed. I can't get up and give you anything.' [8] I tell you, even though he will not get up and give you the bread because of friendship, yet because of your shameless audacity he will surely get up and give you as much as you need.
>
> [9] "So I say to you: Ask and it will be given to you; seek and you will find; knock and the door will be opened to you. [10] For everyone who asks receives; the one who seeks finds; and to the one who knocks, the door will be opened.
>
> **Luke 11:5–10**

I. Other than the Lord's Prayer, what verses or passages from God's Word have you prayed before? How has praying based on Scripture helped you focus your time in talking to God?

Ps. 90:1   Ps 91   Ps 86:12   Eph 4:29   Eph 3:16-15
Eph 1:17 76

2. What other biblically based plans, such as devotionals or Bible studies, have you used to enhance your prayer life? Which have been effective in helping you prioritize prayer?

3. Why do you think Jesus followed up his instruction on how to pray with this exhortation to "ask, seek, and knock" (see verse 9)? Based on your experience and observations, how do the two—praying and asking—go together?

4. What current needs and petitions have you recently been bringing before the Lord? What are your expectations about God's response to your requests?

5. When have you prayed audacious requests and experienced God's solution, provision, or blessing? Did he answer your prayers gradually over time or immediately and dramatically?

6. Read through the passage above once more and then write it out as a prayer below. Ask God to help you understand, appreciate, and practice prayer like never before.

— DAY 3 —
CULTIVATE A LIFESTYLE OF PRAYER

Read the excerpt below from *Pray First*, and then answer the questions that follow.

> God wants us to view prayer as the vibrant foundation of our relationship with him. A lifestyle of prayer is the secret to an authentic Christian life. How do we make prayer a lifestyle? By weaving it into the fabric of our daily lives as we make it the priority God intended. Once we realize how talking and listening to God draws us closer, we enjoy the intimacy we've longed to experience. We know the peace that passes all human understanding (see Philippians 4:7) and take shelter in the unconditional love (see Romans 8:38–39) of our heavenly Father. . . . Prayer empowers us to live supernaturally. Relying on our relationship with God is the only way to accomplish all that he has created us to do in this life. Prayer is necessary because God calls us to do things that we can never accomplish on our own.[1]

I. When have you experienced true intimacy with God through prayer? Looking back, what strikes you about the way you communicated with God and he with you?

2. What benefits have you experienced in your life from relying on prayer? How do these benefits affect your everyday life?

3. Complete the following sentences:

Prayer is essential to my life because . . .

Prayer is essential to my relationship with God because . . .

— DAY 4 —
TAKE INVENTORY

Today your assignment is to really think through each of these fundamentals of prayer. Complete the following prayer inventory to help you assess how each of the *P*'s that we've covered in this session can be implemented or improved in your life.

PRIORITY

I. Before beginning this study, how often did you regularly pray?

2. How often would you like to pray—keeping in mind all your daily responsibilities?

3. What can you change—in your mindset, your schedule, your routines—to make prayer a greater priority in your life?

PLACE

I. Where do you tend to pray most often in your home? In other places?

2. What spot in your home or office can you designate as your new place of regular prayer?

3. What can you do to make this place conducive to spending time with God?

PLAN

I. What kinds of prayer plans, if any, have you tried in the past? What have you learned about which plans help more than hinder your prayer time?

2. Scan the prayer models in section 2 of *Pray First.* Which catches your attention? Explain your response.

3. Contact someone from your group before your next session and ask them what prayer plans they recommend. Write down their responses in the space below.

POWER

1. How often when you pray do you expect to receive the supernatural power of God? How often *should* you expect to access his divine power?

2. What kind of power from God do you need right now in your life?

3. How do you sense the power of the Holy Spirit at work in your life right now? What do you sense that you being empowered to do for God's kingdom?

PERSON

1. Which of the three Persons of the Godhead is hardest for you to relate to? Explain your response.

2. In what ways do you think your experiences with your earthly father(s) have influenced your ability to relate to God as your Abba Father?

3. Which Person of the Trinity do you feel drawn to spend more time with in prayer?

— DAY 5 —
TAKE ACTION

Now that you have completed the prayer inventory and reflected on each of the five *P*'s, it's time to get personal, practical, and productive about how you're going to use them in your prayer life.

First review each *P* below and then answer the questions that follow.

- **Priority.** Starting each day with prayer is paramount to keeping it your priority. Even if you're not a morning person or have urgent demands and distractions pulling at you before you're out of bed, praying first begins with the first moments of your day. Simply put, God wants to be first—in your affection, attention, attitude, and actions.

- **Place.** Having a designated place conducive to prayer aids in consistency. Setting matters! Where you pray regularly matters and can facilitate your ability to focus on God without interruption or distraction. Remember that Jesus had special places to pray . . . and you need one too.

- **Plan.** Having a plan will make a huge difference in the quality of your time with God. Prayer plans free you up to stay focused on what matters most and prevent you from neglecting certain aspects of your relationship with God. Having a prayer plan will help you take your time with God seriously.

- **Power.** The most powerful force on earth is God's power in answering the prayers of his people. Prayer prevails when nothing else works. Powerful prayers are unified, Scriptural, and bold. They unleash heaven on earth.

- **Person.** Prayer revolves around intimacy with God as three-Persons-in-One: the Trinity. Each Person in the Godhead has a distinct role. One of the best descriptions of these unique roles can be found 2 Corinthians 13:14: "The amazing grace of the Master, Jesus Christ, the extravagant love of God, the intimate friendship of the Holy Spirit, be with all of you" (MSG).

What specific changes will you implement immediately to focus on . . .

The **priority** for prayer:

The **place** of prayer:

The **plan** for prayer:

The **power** you seek in prayer:

Your relationship to each **Person** of the Godhead in prayer:

FOR NEXT WEEK | Before you meet with your group next week, read chapter 6 in *Pray First.* (Also consider reading chapter 7 to learn about the prayer of Moses.) Read Matthew 6:9–13 and begin thinking about how to view the Lord's Prayer in a fresh way—one that helps you prioritize and focus your own prayers. Complete any of the study and reflection questions from this personal study that you weren't able to finish.

schedule

WEEK 2

BEFORE GROUP MEETING	Read the Introduction and chapters 1–5 in *Pray First* Read the Welcome section (page 30)
GROUP MEETING	Discuss the Connect questions Watch the video teaching for session 2 Discuss the questions that follow as a group Do the closing exercise and pray (pages 30–40)
PERSONAL STUDY – DAY 1	Complete the daily study (pages 42–44)
PERSONAL STUDY – DAY 2	Complete the daily study (pages 45–47)
PERSONAL STUDY – DAY 3	Complete the daily study (pages 48–49)
PERSONAL STUDY – DAY 4	Complete the daily study (pages 50–51)
PERSONAL STUDY – DAY 5 (BEFORE WEEK 3 GROUP MEETING)	Read chapter 6 in *Pray First* Complete any unfinished personal studies (pages 52–53)

the Lord's prayer

It's important to realize that Jesus wasn't teaching us words to memorize but rather how to connect with our Father.

CHRIS HODGES

WELCOME | READ ON YOUR OWN

The Lord's Prayer is one of the most familiar passages in the Bible. It is taught in children's Sunday school and catechism classes across a spectrum of faith denominations. It's often recited during church services, at weddings and funerals, and in various group settings. But the Lord's Prayer is more than a passage to recite. It's an expansive model for how to pray.

The disciples of Jesus, like all Jewish boys in their day, would have learned and recited prayers from an early age. But when they heard Jesus communicate with his heavenly Father, they recognized that something was different. Their Master wasn't praying like they had been taught. This is why the disciples asked their Teacher to show them how to do it his way.

In answering their request, Jesus used a technique that Jewish rabbis commonly used—teaching God's truth through the use of an outline. His model prayer, commonly called the Lord's Prayer, contains seven topics that continue to instruct us on how to pray today.

In providing this instructive model prayer, Jesus wasn't teaching us words to memorize but revealing how we should connect with our heavenly Father. Similar to the way in which the rabbinical teaching of the day followed specific outlines, Jesus concisely demonstrated elements for us to explore and expand on as we pray. These elements provide a timeless method for connecting fully with God and addressing the priorities of every believer.

CONNECT | 15 MINUTES

If you or any of your group members don't know each other, take a few minutes to introduce yourselves. Then choose one of the following questions to discuss as a group:

- What is a key insight or takeaway from last week's personal study that you would like to share with the group?

  — or —

- How often do you use the Lord's Prayer as part of your personal prayer time?

WATCH | 20 MINUTES

Now it's time to watch the video for this session (remember that you can access this video via streaming by following the instructions printed on the inside front cover). As you watch, use the following outline to record any thoughts or concepts that stand out to you.

I. Connect with God relationally

    A. "Our Father in heaven" (Matthew 6:9a NKJV). Calling God our Father allows us to connect with him relationally.

    B. When we call God our Father, we use his favorite title, which reflects his lavish love for us.

    C. Your view of God will determine your relationship with God.

II. Worship his name

    A. "Hallowed be Your name" (verse 9b NKJV). In Proverbs 18:10, we read that God's name is a place of protection for the righteous. We can actually run to his name to find safety.

    B. The names of God in Scripture are important because the name of God is the power of God. Demons bow at the name of Jesus (see Philippians 2:10–11).

    C. In the heavenlies, the name of God carries weight, authority, and power.

III. Pray God's agenda first

    A. "Your kingdom come. Your will be done on earth as it is in heaven" (verse 10 NKJV). The Bible says that when we go to God in prayer, we pray for *his* kingdom to come and *his* will to be done.

B. God will always give you what you need from day to day if you will make the kingdom of God your primary concern (see Luke 12:31).

C. God's agenda is always people. It's even people who are far from him, people who are hurting, and people who have never heard the gospel.

IV. Depend on God for everything

A. "Give us this day our daily bread" (verse 11 NKJV). When we pray this and say, "give us," we're communicating that God has everything we need.

B. It's good for us to ask God for things that we think we can take care of ourselves. We don't wait until we've lost them to ask God for them.

C. Be specific and ask God for everything that you need in your life.

V. Get your heart right with God and people

A. "Forgive us our debts, as we forgive our debtors" (verse 12 NKJV). First, we confess to God that we have some attitudes or some issues in our lives that are not pleasing to him.

B. When we confess our sins daily to God and ask him to search our hearts, it keeps us from getting desensitized to the world and to the impact of our sins.

C. We also must get our hearts right with people. Every day, forgive the people who have hurt you and, in your mind, forgive those who *will* hurt you that day.

VI. Engage in spiritual warfare

    A. "And do not lead us into temptation, but deliver us from the evil one" (verse 13a NKJV). Prayer is not just communion with God but also confrontation with the enemy.

    B. The enemy's greatest weapon is a lie. He will lie to you about your identity, about your future, about your problems—even about God. Make your declarations against him out of God's Word.

    C. Every day, take your stand against the enemy and fight the good fight of faith.

VII. Express faith in God's ability

    A. "For yours is the kingdom and the power and the glory forever" (verse 13b NKJV). We release our faith by reminding ourselves of God's ability and limitless power.

B. It's a great exclamation point at the end of our prayer time to acknowledge that nothing is too difficult for God.

C. If you use the Lord's Prayer as a process to follow, you will enjoy prayer at a whole new level.

DISCUSS | 35 MINUTES

Discuss what you just watched by answering the following questions as time allows.

I. The first line of the Lord's Prayer reads: "Our Father in heaven, hallowed be Your name" (Matthew 6:9). What challenges have you faced in viewing God as your loving Father? What has helped you to see him more clearly in this way?

2. The next portion of the Lord's Prayer reads: "Your kingdom come, your will be done, on earth as it is in heaven" (verse 10). Why do you think Jesus included this instruction to pray for God's kingdom to come on earth? What does it mean to pray for God's will to be done?

3. Jesus' next instruction in his model prayer is simply: "Give us today our daily bread" (verse 11). What is the significance in asking for God to provide our *daily* bread? When you ask God to provide your "daily bread," what are you usually including?

4. The final section of the Lord's Prayer reads: "And forgive us our debts, as we also have forgiven our debtors. And lead us not into temptation, but deliver us from the evil one" (verses 12-13). How frequently do you use prayer to confront the enemy? How does prayer help you overcome the devil's temptations, snares, and deceptions?

5. Have you ever considered the Lord's Prayer as being a *model* for prayer rather than a particular prayer to memorize and recite? How would you explain the difference?

6. Which of the seven aspects of the Lord's Prayer that were covered in this session resonates with you most right now? Why does that particular aspect stand out to you?

7. The word *hallow* means "to make holy or set apart for holy use."[2] What does it mean for you to hallow God's name? What aspects of God's name mean the most to you?

8. How will praying The Lord's Prayer be different for you moving forward? How can you personalize it while maintaining the seven components that we've discussed in this session?

RESPOND | 10 MINUTES

In the video for this week's teaching, we focused on the Lord's Prayer as recorded in Matthew's Gospel. Now take a few minutes on your own to read this prayer as it is recorded in Luke's Gospel. When you are finished reading, answer the questions that follow.

> 2 "Father,
> hallowed be your name,
> your kingdom come.
> 3 Give us each day our daily bread.
> 4 Forgive us our sins,
> for we also forgive everyone who sins against us.
> And lead us not into temptation."
>
> **Luke 11:2–4**

What similar words and phrases are found in each version of the prayer?

What are some of the differences found in each version of the prayer?

What confuses you, concerns you, or piques your curiosity in this prayer model?

PRAY | 10 MINUTES

Wrap up your group's time by praying together, asking each person to pray aloud using one of these seven topics of the Lord's Prayer. Try not to rush through this process as you explore each of these seven aspects, including praise and worship, provision, forgiveness and grace, and protection and power. Thank Jesus for providing this outline to help you draw closer to your heavenly Father. Finally, use the space below to write down any requests mentioned so that you and your group members can continue to pray about them in the week ahead.

Name　　　　Request

personal
STUDY

In your group time this week, you explored a technique that Jesus used to teach his disciples how to pray in the way they had witnessed him praying. This model prayer was not intended to teach them words to memorize but to provide them with an effective way of connecting with their heavenly Father each day. In this personal study, you will continue to explore the Lord's Prayer and create a plan for incorporating it into your prayer life. Be sure to write down your responses to the questions in the spaces provided, as you will be given a few minutes to share your insights at the start of the next session if you are doing this study with others. If you are reading *Pray First* alongside this study, first review chapter 6 in the book.

— DAY 1 —
PRAY FIRST

Sometimes, being too familiar with the Lord's Prayer can be an obstacle in reconsidering it as a model for how you should pray. You may feel so locked in to the way you learned it, the time you learned it, or the translation in which you learned it, that your mind automatically goes on autopilot, like reciting the Pledge of Allegiance or your home address.

Comparing different versions of a familiar passage from Scripture can give you a fresh perspective on its meaning. While translating the ancient, original languages of God's Word has always presented challenges, it also provides unique benefits. Most biblical translations attempt to find balance between the idea or message of the original text and expressing God's truth with stylistic elements, such as word choice, sentence structure, and metaphors. Especially with well-known verses and passages, you may discover a richer perspective on God's Word by noting the differences between translations.

The Lord's Prayer is at the top of most lists of well-known passages from the Bible, so it's an especially good candidate for making such comparisons. Keep this goal in mind as you read the two versions of the Lord's Prayer below. The first is drawn from one of the oldest and most famous translations, the King James Version, while the second comes from a more contemporary paraphrase, *The Message*. Read through both versions slowly and thoughtfully, underlining key words and phrases you want to compare between them. Use the questions that follow to help you gain a fresh perspective on this timeless model of how to pray.

> [9] Our Father which art in heaven, Hallowed be thy name.
> [10] Thy kingdom come, Thy will be done in earth, as it is in heaven.
> [11] Give us this day our daily bread.
> [12] And forgive us our debts, as we forgive our debtors.
> [13] And lead us not into temptation, but deliver us from evil: For thine is the kingdom, and the power, and the glory, for ever. Amen.
>
> **Matthew 6:9–13 KJV**

⁹ Our Father in heaven,
Reveal who you are.
¹⁰ Set the world right;
Do what's best—
   as above, so below.
¹¹ Keep us alive with three square meals.
¹² Keep us forgiven with you and forgiving others.
¹³ Keep us safe from ourselves and the Devil.
You're in charge!
You can do anything you want!
You're ablaze in beauty!
   Yes. Yes. Yes.

Matthew 6:9–13 MSG

I. Which particular words or phrases did you underline in each of these translations? How do those words or phrases compare between the two versions?

2. What is the greatest difference between these two versions of the Lord's Prayer?

3. Does one version resonate with you and your present faith journey more than the other? What resonates with you about that version's wording of the prayer?

4. What surprises you most about the ways these different versions express the same ideas?

5. Now choose another translation besides the New International Version, the King James Version, or The Message. Look up this same passage and read it through several times. What else stands out to you after comparing that translation to the versions that you've already read?

6. Does comparing versions change the way you view the Lord's Prayer? Why or why not?

— DAY 2 —
PRAY GOD'S WORD

As you begin rethinking the Lord's Prayer and how you can more fully incorporate it into all areas of your life, you may encounter resistance, both from within yourself and from external circumstances. Keep in mind that the enemy wants to sabotage anything that draws you closer to God and helps you grow spiritually. This is especially true when it comes to prayer.

The devil is always plotting, scheming, and working to bring about your downfall. As the apostle Peter warns, "Be alert and of sober mind. Your enemy the devil prowls around like a roaring lion looking for someone to devour" (1 Peter 5:8). If you are not fighting off the devil every day, then he is working harder than you are!

Prayer is first and foremost communion with God, but it's also confrontation with the devil. As Paul writes, "For our struggle is not against flesh and blood, but against the rulers, against the authorities, against the powers of this dark world and against the spiritual forces of evil in the heavenly realms" (Ephesians 6:12). When you pray, you take your stand against the enemy.

Confronting the enemy means casting down his lies—everything that is not aligned with God's will—and replacing it with God's truth. Spiritual warfare is about binding the devil and his schemes against you and your family and those you love in the name of Jesus. It means standing strong in the protective authority of your heavenly Father.

But you are far from defenseless! You can adapt a number of spiritual warfare prayers from Scripture when you or someone you know is under attack from the devil. Knowing that you are in a spiritual battle, God provides spiritual armor and equips you to take a stand when battles come your way. Begin today to take up the protection God that has given you by praying through the different pieces of armor described in the following passage. Use the questions that follow to help you form a prayer-based strategy for overcoming the enemy.

> [11] Put on the full armor of God, so that you can take your stand against the devil's schemes. [12] For our struggle is not against flesh and blood, but against the rulers, against the authorities, against the powers of this dark world and against the spiritual forces of evil in the heavenly realms. [13] Therefore put on the full armor of God, so that when the day of evil comes, you may be able to stand your ground, and after you have done everything, to stand. [14] Stand firm then, with the belt of truth buckled around your waist, with the breastplate of righteousness in place, [15] and with your feet fitted with the readiness that comes from the gospel of peace. [16] In addition to all this, take up the shield of faith, with which you can extinguish all the flaming arrows of the evil one. [17] Take the helmet of salvation and the sword of the Spirit, which is the word of God. [18] And pray in the Spirit on all occasions with all kinds of prayers and requests. With this in mind, be alert and always keep on praying for all the Lord's people.
>
> **Ephesians 6:11–18**

I. How does putting on the full armor of God help you overcome the devil's schemes?

2. Of the various pieces of armor listed, which do you need most at present in your life? Why?

3. How does prayer help you to stand your ground against the enemy and his temptations?

4. According to this passage, which piece of armor can extinguish all the arrows of the evil one? How would you describe this piece of armor in your own life?

5. What does it mean for you to "pray in the Spirit"? What do you see as the Holy Spirit's role when you engage in spiritual warfare?

6. Using this passage as your basis, write a brief prayer of spiritual warfare that you can pray each day. Feel free to bring your circumstances, personal situations, and relationships into the prayer. Make this prayer a kind of battle cry as you overcome the snares of the devil and experience the victory and freedom you have in Christ.

— DAY 3 —
CULTIVATE A LIFESTYLE OF PRAYER

Read the excerpt below from chapter 6 of *Pray First*, and then answer the questions that follow.

> When his disciples asked him to teach them to pray, Jesus used a technique that many rabbis used—teaching God's truth by providing an outline drawn from the Scriptures. The disciples already knew how to pray based on their upbringing. They had learned traditional prayers that most Jewish males memorized as part of their upbringing.
>
> But when they saw and heard Jesus pray, they were stunned. He wasn't praying as they had been taught, so they asked their Master to teach them to do it his way. So that's exactly what Jesus did—he gave them the gift of an outline for how to talk to the Father. It changed everything for the disciples that day . . .
>
> While we'll explore several distinct models found in the Bible, the best starting point is the prayer outline Jesus himself gave us. It's the model prayer of all model prayers. . . . But it's important to realize that Jesus wasn't teaching us words to memorize but rather how to connect with our Father. With this relational goal in mind, Christ gave us an outline with seven distinct aspects of prayer. Similar to rabbinical teaching of the day that followed specific outlines, Jesus concisely demonstrated elements for us to explore and expand upon as we pray.[3]

I. Do you recall when you first encountered or memorized the Lord's Prayer? What impressions and assumptions about this prayer have you carried with you throughout your life?

2. How does viewing this prayer as a *model* rather than a *prayer to memorize* change your understanding of why Jesus taught his followers to pray this way?

3. Why do you think Jesus used a common rabbinical teaching method of that time to instruct his followers to pray in such a radical new way?

— DAY 4 —
TAKE INVENTORY

Rewrite each of the following key phrases of the Lord's Prayer from the New King James Version in the kind of conversational language you use today.

I. Our Father in heaven . . .

2. Hallowed be Your name . . .

3. Your kingdom come. Your will be done on earth as it is in heaven . . .

4. Give us this day our daily bread . . .

5. And forgive us our debts, as we forgive our debtors . . .

6. And do not lead us into temptation, but deliver us from the evil one . . .

7. For Yours is the kingdom and the power and the glory forever . . .

— DAY 5 —
TAKE ACTION

It's no coincidence that Jesus offered his prayer model to a *group* of his disciples—as praying the seven aspects of the Lord's Prayer works well not only for individuals but also for groups. Throughout the New Testament, we find references to believers in the early church praying together, fulfilling what Jesus had told his followers:

> [18] "Truly I tell you, whatever you bind on earth will be bound in heaven, and whatever you loose on earth will be loosed in heaven. [19] Again, truly I tell you that if two of you on earth agree about anything they ask for, it will be done for them by my Father in heaven. [20] For where two or three gather in my name, there am I with them."
>
> **Matthew 18:18–20**

Arrange to meet with someone this week to pray together. This can be someone from your group, someone you know well and have previously prayed with together, or a believer you would like to know better. Try to meet for at least an hour. Spend the first few minutes getting better acquainted, then share personal prayer requests, and then spend the rest of your time lifting up your hearts to God. Pray through each of the seven items in the Lord's Prayer you've been learning about this week. Make a plan to meet and pray together again if possible. Take a few moments after your time together to reflect on the following questions.

I. What stood out to you about this time you spent praying with the other person?

2. How was this experience different from when you pray on your own?

3. How easy or difficult was it for you to use the Lord's Prayer as your model for this time?

FOR NEXT WEEK| Before you meet with your group next week, read chapter 6 in *Pray First*. (Also consider reading chapter 7 to learn about the prayer of Moses.) Read 1 Chronicles 4:9–10 and begin thinking about what this passage says about Jabez and the content of his prayer. Go back and complete any of the study and reflection questions from this personal study that you weren't able to finish.

schedule

WEEK 3

BEFORE GROUP MEETING	Read chapter 8 in *Pray First* Read the Welcome section (page 56)
GROUP MEETING	Discuss the Connect questions Watch the video teaching for session 3 Discuss the questions that follow as a group Do the closing exercise and pray (pages 56–64)
PERSONAL STUDY – DAY 1	Complete the daily study (pages 66–68)
PERSONAL STUDY – DAY 2	Complete the daily study (pages 69–71)
PERSONAL STUDY – DAY 3	Complete the daily study (pages 72–73)
PERSONAL STUDY – DAY 4	Complete the daily study (pages 74–75)
PERSONAL STUDY – DAY 5 (BEFORE WEEK 4 GROUP MEETING)	Read chapter 9 in *Pray First* Complete any unfinished personal studies (pages 76–77)

the prayer of Jabez

Jabez wasn't willing to settle for a life of pain—and neither should you.

CHRIS HODGES

WELCOME | READ ON YOUR OWN

Many people have names that stick with them throughout their entire lives. This name might be a variation of their proper name that was given to them at birth or—as is more often the case—a nickname derived from a trait, quality, or role they played growing up. (This explains why you might know a Shorty, Lefty, Precious, or Joker.)

In ancient times, a person's name often carried even *more* weight. It sometimes revealed circumstances that were occurring at the time of the person's birth or the expectations that others held for him or her. As we look at Scripture, these names can seem prophetic at times as we witness the person grow into the name he or she has been given. Such is the case for a man mentioned only briefly in the Bible but who provides a timeless prayer model: *Jabez*.

The name Jabez sounds similar to the Hebrew word for pain. He had received this name from his mother, who explained, "I gave birth to him in pain" (1 Chronicles 4:9). But Jabez refused to become a victim of this troubling label given to him at birth. Although his story—and his well-known prayer—are contained within only a couple of verses, he reminds us that how we pray influences *who we are* and *who we become*.

The prayer of Jabez reveals how to overcome pain and suffering by being deliberate about what we pray. His example demonstrates that instead of being bound by painful labels given to us in the past, we can forge ahead and ask God to bless us, be with us, and keep us in his care and loving embrace. Jabez wasn't willing to settle for a life of pain. Neither should we.

CONNECT | 15 MINUTES

Get the session started by choosing one of the following questions to discuss as a group:

- What is a key insight or takeaway from last week's personal study that you would like to share with the group?

  — or —

- Did you have a nickname growing up? If so, would you care to share it?

WATCH | 20 MINUTES

Now watch the video for this session. As you go through the material, use the following outline to record any thoughts or concepts that stand out to you.

I. Pray for blessing

    A. "Oh, that you would bless me" (1 Chronicles 4:10a). In the Hebrew, the word for *blessing* is *prosper,* which means to be pushed forward further than we would be able to get on our own.

    B. We pray for God's blessing so that we can be a blessing to others. *Lord, give me more than I need so I can be a blessing to the world around me.*

    C. Real biblical prosperity is not health and wealth, name it and claim it, blab it and grab it. It's having more than we need so we can make an eternal difference in the lives of others.

II. Pray for influence

    A. "Enlarge my territory" (verse 10b). Once God gives us his blessing, he wants us to take that blessing and use it to make a difference in other people's lives.

    B. Our inheritance is other people. We don't literally possess them or own them, but we have influence in their lives by being a blessing to them.

    C. If the size of your dream isn't intimidating to you, there's a good chance that it is insulting to God. *Lord, use me so that my life might make an eternal impact in the lives of others.*

III. Pray for presence

    A. "Let your hand be with me" (verse 10c). The hand of the Lord is a biblical term used throughout Scripture for God's presence and God's power.

    B. If God gives you more than you need (blessing) and gives you influence, you're going to feel in over your head. You're going to need God's presence in your life.

    C. God blesses you, gives you influence, and then anoints you so that you can do what he has called you to do. *Lord, be with me because what you've called me to is too big for me.*

IV. Pray for protection

A. "Keep me from evil" (verse 10d NKJV). If you have blessing, you can use it to influence; and if you have God's hand upon you, all of hell is not going to like it. We need God's protection.

B. Some of us are under attack right now. We sense that the enemy has come against God's call and plan on our lives. So what do we do? We pray for God's protection.

C. Philippians 2:10 says that every demonic principality has to bow at the name of Jesus. *Lord, strengthen me and rescue me from every attack of the enemy.*

DISCUSS | 35 MINUTES

Discuss what you just watched by answering the following questions as time allows.

I. Jabez began his prayer with this request: "Oh, that you would bless me" (1 Chronicles 4:10a). Do you agree that the concept of *blessing* is often misunderstood? How would you define or describe blessing based on what's in God's Word?

2. Jabez then prayed, "[God], enlarge my territory" (verse 10b). Jabez was asking God for influence in making this request. What does having influence mean to you? What are some ways God is presently using you to influence the lives of those around you?

3. Jabez then said to God, "Let your hand be with me" (verse 10c). As you receive blessing and exert influence, why does praying for God's *presence* become more urgent?

4. Jabez concluded with this request: "Keep me from harm so that I will be free from pain" (verse 10d). Why is seeking God's *protection* from the enemy necessary in light of experiencing his blessing, influence, and presence in your life?

5. Of these four prayer items, which one have you sometimes overlooked in the past when praying? How does the prayer of Jabez remind you to focus on all four?

6. Considering the way in which you typically pray to the Lord, would you say that your focus has been more on what *you* want or what *God* wants? Explain.

7. When and how has God blessed you in order that you could bless others? What did you learn about him from this experience?

8. What did you know about the Prayer of Jabez before this session? How has your understanding of the prayer now changed?

RESPOND | 10 MINUTES

As mentioned in the video, the entire story of Jabez and his prayer is contained in just two verses in the Bible. In a genealogical list of 600 names in the book of 1 Chronicles, this man is singled out—and mentioned nowhere else in Scripture. Take a few moments on your own to read the concise story of Jabez and then answer the questions that follow.

> [9] Jabez was more honorable than his brothers. His mother had named him Jabez, saying, "I gave birth to him in pain." [10] Jabez cried out to the God of Israel, "Oh, that you would bless me and enlarge my territory! Let your hand be with me, and keep me from harm so that I will be free from pain." And God granted his request.
>
> **1 Chronicles 4:9–10**

Why do you think we are told that Jabez was more honorable than his brothers *before* we learn the meaning of his name?

What stands out to you the most about the prayer of Jabez? Why?

Why do you think the writer includes the detail that God answered his prayer?

PRAY | 10 MINUTES

Go around the group and allow each person to share personal prayer requests. Then spend a few minutes praying together using the four categories—blessing, influence, presence, and protection—found in the Prayer of Jabez. Thank God for all that you are learning about prayer in order to learn more about him. Ask him to focus the eyes of your heart on what he focuses on—people and their needs. Praise him for this study and the fellowship you are experiencing in your group. Use the space below to write down any requests mentioned so that you and your group members can continue to pray about them in the week ahead.

Name   Request

personal
STUDY

In your group time this week, you explored a short prayer found in just two verses in the book of 1 Chronicles that reveals how to pray for God's blessing, influence, presence, and protection. Now that you're becoming aware of some of these different types of prayer models found in Scripture, begin using them to change the way you spend your time with God each day. Think about the aspects of prayer that resonate most with you and how you can use these various kinds of prayers to expand your ways of communicating with the Lord. Be sure to write down your responses to the questions in the spaces provided, as you will be given a few minutes to share your insights at the start of the next session if you are doing this study with others. If you are reading *Pray First* alongside this study, first review chapter 8 in the book.

— DAY 1 —
PRAY FIRST

Many people, both those inside and outside the church, misunderstand the concept of God's *blessing*. Some assume it's all about health and wealth, naming and claiming it, blab it and grab it . . . gaining all the material and physical benefits this life has to offer. However, based on the way *God* defines blessing, it's simply about his supernatural favor, an abundance in every area of our lives that exceeds our expectations—and sometimes our imaginations.

This is the kind of blessing that Jabez requested, and it is the kind of blessing that you should request as well. After all, any material or physical gain pales next to the joy, peace, purpose, and contentment that come from experiencing the lavish love of your heavenly Father. And your Father blesses you not so that you can accumulate riches, escape economic limitations, or experience comfort and convenience, but so that you—as his conduit—can pour yourself into the lives of others. As his Word clearly explains, "I will bless you . . . and you will be a blessing to others" (Genesis 12:2 NLT).

You are blessed to be a blessing. God doesn't bless you so that you can feel secure, compensated, or superior to others. Rather, he entrusts you to steward the resources that he has provided so that others will come to know him and experience the love of Christ. Seen from this perspective, if you're *not* blessed, your ability to bless others is limited! Keep this principle in mind as you read the passage below and then answer the questions that follow.

> [14] Satisfy us in the morning with your unfailing love,
>   that we may sing for joy and be glad all our days.
> [15] Make us glad for as many days as you have afflicted us,
>   for as many years as we have seen trouble.
> [16] May your deeds be shown to your servants,
>   your splendor to their children.
> [17] May the favor of the Lord our God rest on us;
>   establish the work of our hands for us—
>   yes, establish the work of our hands.
>
> **Psalm 90:14-17**

I. Based only on what you learned growing up, how would you define *blessing*? How has your understanding of its meaning changed over your lifetime?

2. When have you experienced a blessing from the Lord that was invisible, intangible, and experiential? How did it help change your definition of blessing?

3. According to the psalmist, who is identified as Moses at the beginning of the text, what are some of the blessings for which you should give thanks?

4. Based on this passage, how do the blessings you receive reflect on God's character? Where do you see evidence of this in the psalm?

5. What are some ways you have experienced the favor of the Lord resting on you in the past year or two? How has this kind of divine favor influenced your view of God?

6. What do you believe it means for God's favor to "establish the work of our hands"? How does God bless us through the work we're called to do?

— DAY 2 —
PRAY GOD'S WORD

Notice that just as Jabez prayed, "Oh, that you would bless me and enlarge my territory!" (1 Chronicles 4:10), *blessing* and *influence* often go together. When you receive God's blessings and use them to bless others, your influence with them naturally increases. They see not only what God has done in your life but also how you've used those blessings for greater causes than your own personal wealth, safety, and comfort.

While this kind of testimony can emerge from how you steward the material blessings God has provided, the gift of his favor may also require you to surrender your plans, expectations, or dreams. Such was the case for a certain young woman, engaged to a respectable man from the town of Nazareth, when an angel appeared to her and announced:

> 28 "Greetings, you who are highly favored! The Lord is with you. . . . 30 Do not be afraid, Mary; you have found favor with God. 31 You will conceive and give birth to a son, and you are to call him Jesus. 32 He will be great and will be called the Son of the Most High. The Lord God will give him the throne of his father David, 33 and he will reign over Jacob's descendants forever; his kingdom will never end."
>
> **Luke 1:28, 30–33**

While Mary must have been taken aback, to say the least, she surrendered her will to God's, telling the angel, "I am the Lord's servant. May your word to me be fulfilled" (Luke 1:38). Not only was Mary willing to receive the favor that God showed by choosing her to be the mother of his Son, but she also trusted God with her body, life, and future. Later, after greeting her cousin Elizabeth, who was also with child (later known as John the Baptist), she proclaimed:

> 46 "My soul glorifies the Lord
> 47 and my spirit rejoices in God my Savior,
> 48 for he has been mindful
> of the humble state of his servant.

> From now on all generations will call me blessed,
> ⁴⁹ for the Mighty One has done great things for me—
> holy is his name.
> ⁵⁰ His mercy extends to those who fear him,
> from generation to generation.
> ⁵¹ He has performed mighty deeds with his arm;
> he has scattered those who are proud in their inmost thoughts.
> ⁵² He has brought down rulers from their thrones
> but has lifted up the humble.
> ⁵³ He has filled the hungry with good things
> but has sent the rich away empty.
> ⁵⁴ He has helped his servant Israel,
> remembering to be merciful
> ⁵⁵ to Abraham and his descendants forever,
> just as he promised our ancestors."
>
> **Luke 1:46–55**

I. What strikes you most about Mary's song of praise to the Lord? What words or phrases particularly connect with you? Circle these in the passage above.

2. Where do you see evidence of both *blessing* and *influence* in Mary's response? How are the two connected in her willingness to be the mother of Jesus?

3. What similarities do you see between Mary's prayer and the prayer of Jabez? How does Mary's song of praise focus more on God than on herself?

4. When have you had to sacrifice your own plans, schedule, wishes, and desires in order to accept a gift from God? What were the consequences of your choice?

5. As you consider the blessings in your life right now, how do they provide you with influence to reflect God's character and advance his kingdom?

6. Read through Mary's song once more so it becomes your prayer. In the space below, express your own praise to God for the purposes he has given you.

— DAY 3 —
CULTIVATE A LIFESTYLE OF PRAYER

Read the excerpt below from chapter 8 of *Pray First*, and then answer the questions that follow.

[Jabez] asked God to impart his supernatural favor and then some. This kind of blessing is on steroids with added exclamation marks! When God stoops down to make us great, our lives overflow with abundance in every area. In fact, God wants to bless us—it's his nature as a Father who lavishly loves his children to pour out his blessings on us. But the reason he blesses us is not so we can be rich and have a lot of stuff and live a life of comfort and leisure. God's Word tells us, "I will bless you . . . and you will be a blessing to others" (Genesis 12:2 NLT). We are blessed to be a blessing! . . .

Many people don't pray this way because they're too focused on their own pain instead of the needs of others. Some ask for blessing but really just want to compensate for past losses or deprivations. They want to feel good about themselves based on their bank accounts or material possessions instead of basing their identity in Jesus Christ. There's nothing wrong with money and possessions, and God often blesses us with them—but not so we can stockpile them for security. The Lord entrusts us to be his stewards and use what we have so that others may know him and experience the love of Jesus.

When I pray for God's blessings, I ask him, "Lord, give me more than I need so that I can be a blessing to the world around me." I'm not telling you this to blow my own horn. I'm simply sharing how I view this prayer request and exercise it accordingly. Pray for blessing so that you can bless others around you.[4]

I. Why do you think Jabez was so bold in asking for God's blessing? Do you agree that the main reason God blesses us is so that we in turn can bless others? Why or why not?

2. When have you been confused or uncertain about what it means for God to bless you? How has your view of God's blessing changed as you have matured in your faith?

3. How are you currently stewarding the blessings that God has given you? How can you bless others more frequently and with greater impact?

— DAY 4 —
TAKE INVENTORY

Jabez prayed succinctly and made four requests of God. Make each of these four requests personal and specific to your situation by completing the statements below.

I. God, I ask for your blessing in this area . . .

2. God, I pray that you would give me greater influence in this area . . .

3. God, as you bless me and give me influence, I pray for your presence to help me . . .

4. God, I pray for your protection in this area as I stand against the enemy . . .

— DAY 5 —
TAKE ACTION

Perhaps one of the reasons the prayer of Jabez works so well as a prayer model is its brevity. As you learned in this week's group session, so much is packed into these two sentences: "Oh, that you would bless me and enlarge my territory! Let your hand be with me, and keep me from harm so that I will be free from pain" (1 Chronicles 4:10).

Because Jabez's prayer is so concise, you can make it your own regardless of whether you only have a minute or ample time to explore all four items—blessing, influence, presence, protection. So, between now and your next group meeting (and beyond, as you feel led), seek to make the prayer of Jabez your default prayer throughout the day. You may want to write it on a note card and keep it with you until you memorize it.

Any time you have a few moments or an unexpected delay, pray what Jabez prayed. When you are waiting at the dentist's office, or on hold with a call for customer service, or stuck in traffic, or sharing coffee with a friend, take a few moments to pray this prayer and make it your own. Then, as time allows, sit in silence for a few moments after praying Jabez's prayer, listening for the whisper of God's Spirit. As praying this prayer becomes a regular habit, remain vigilant and look for signs of God's blessing, influence, presence, and protection.

Finally, take a few moments at the end of the day to reflect on the following questions.

I.   How successful were you in making the prayer of Jabez your own throughout the day? What challenges and/or distractions did you face?

2. How was praying this prayer throughout the day different from the way in which you normally pray?

3. What did you sense the Holy Spirit was saying to you as you sat in silence?

FOR NEXT WEEK | Before you meet again with your group next week, read chapter 9 in *Pray First.* (Also consider reading chapter 10 to learn about the prayers for the lost.) Read Psalm 23 and begin thinking about what this passage says about God and how he cares for us. In addition, make sure to go back and complete any of the study and reflection questions from this personal study that you weren't able to finish.

schedule

WEEK 4

BEFORE GROUP MEETING	Read chapter 9 in *Pray First* Read the Welcome section (page 80)
GROUP MEETING	Discuss the Connect questions Watch the video teaching for session 4 Discuss the questions that follow as a group Do the closing exercise and pray (pages 80–90)
PERSONAL STUDY – DAY 1	Complete the daily study (pages 92–94)
PERSONAL STUDY – DAY 2	Complete the daily study (pages 95–97)
PERSONAL STUDY – DAY 3	Complete the daily study (pages 98–99)
PERSONAL STUDY – DAY 4	Complete the daily study (pages 100–101)
PERSONAL STUDY – DAY 5 (BEFORE WEEK 5 GROUP MEETING)	Read chapter 12 in *Pray First* Complete any unfinished personal studies (pages 102–103)

praying the names of God

Instead of focusing on ourselves, praying the names of God makes it all about him.

CHRIS HODGES

WELCOME | READ ON YOUR OWN

Have you ever had a conversation with someone that seemed more like a monologue? As they bounce from topic to topic, you're barely able to utter a response—"*uh huh, right, yeah*"—before they're off to their next story, observation, or rant. They may not even realize that they are completely monopolizing the conversation unless you interrupt them.

Our prayers to God can become like these one-sided conversations. When we jump right into our thoughts, feelings, and requests, it's all about what God can do for *us* rather than what we can do for *God*. Such lopsided prayers overlook who God is and what he wants to say to us.

This is the value of this next model of prayer that we will cover in this session. Instead of focusing on ourselves, praying the names of God makes it all about him. These prayers help us to focus on God's character, qualities, and abilities. We humble ourselves in his presence and give our full attention to him. When we then make our requests and petitions known, we are communicating confidence in who he is and not merely in what he can do for us.

Praying the names of God helps us to get the order straight—and put God first in our lives and in our day. When we approach him on his terms, not our own, we make it clear that we want to know all aspects of God and the fullness of his character. Praying this way pleases the Lord, while helping us to know more of who he is and what he is truly like.

CONNECT | 15 MINUTES

Get the session started by choosing one of the following questions to discuss as a group:

- What is a key insight or takeaway from last week's personal study that you would like to share with the group?

  — *or* —

- Do you enjoy making small talk with people, or do you prefer deeper conversations? Why?

WATCH | 20 MINUTES

Now watch the video for this session. As you go through the material, use the following outline to record any thoughts or concepts that stand out to you.

I. You are my Shepherd

A. "The LORD is my shepherd" (Psalm 23:1a NKJV). The word *shepherd* literally means *pastor.* God is watching over us and pastoring us as we go through this life.

B. Jesus is the Chief Shepherd. In John 10:4, we read that Jesus said we are like sheep and he is the shepherd. The sheep recognize his voice and turn away from the voice of the enemy.

II. You are my Provider

A. "I shall not want" (verse 1b NKJV). We literally will not lack because God is watching over our lives. We will never be in need or "begging for bread," because God is the provider in our lives.

B. We trust God to provide, so we give him the first of everything. We tithe, and give, and go to church on the first day of the week. We give to him first, knowing that he will provide the rest.

III. You are my Peace

A. "He makes me to lie down in green pastures; He leads me beside the still waters" (verse 2 NKJV). Even in the middle of anxiety, fear, chaos, worry, stress, and depression, God is our peace.

B. God will keep us in perfect peace because we have our minds stayed on him and trust in him, knowing that he is guarding our soul.

IV. You are my Healer

    A. "He restores my soul" (verse 3a NKJV). To *restore* means to return something back to the point of departure. God brings everything that got undone back to the original point of departure.

    B. A *disease* is every place where you are dis-eased. So we pray for God to bring healing not only in our physical bodies but also in every area of our lives that needs his touch..

V. You are my Righteousness

    A. "He leads me in the paths of righteousness for His name's sake" (verse 3b NKJV). When we are saved, we are made completely new and completely clean. We are made righteous before God.

B. But God still leads us on the paths of righteousness. We thank God that we are no longer where we used to be, but we want to keep growing in righteousness. We want to be more like Christ.

VI. You are my Constant Companion

A. "Yea, though I walk through the valley of the shadow of death, I will fear no evil; for You are with me; Your rod and Your staff, they comfort me" (verse 4 NKJV). In the Old Testament, God was literally called "THE LORD IS THERE" (see Ezekiel 48:35).

B. In the New Testament, the Holy Spirit is described as the Comforter who will abide with us forever. He will be right alongside us and help us through life.

VII. You are my Defender

    A. "You prepare a table before me in the presence of my enemies" (verse 5a NKJV). We don't have to fight our own battles. We can sit at a table and eat because God is fighting our battles for us.

    B. Right now there are men and women engaged in battles around the world to defend our freedoms. God is doing the same. He is fighting battles that we don't even know anything about.

VIII. You are my Sanctifier

    A. "You anoint my head with oil; my cups runs over" (verse 5b NKJV). God anoints us and gives us more than we need so we can be a blessing to the world around us.

B. The word *sanctify* in the Greek literally means to be set apart for a special work. God sanctifies us, or sets us apart, so that we can be used by him in a great way.

DISCUSS | 35 MINUTES

Discuss what you just watched by answering the following questions as time allows.

1. "The LORD is my shepherd" (Psalm 23:1a). How has God "shepherded" you in life? How do you tend to respond when you sense that he is leading you?

2. "I lack nothing" (verse 1b). How easy or difficult is it for you to trust that God will provide for your needs? How are you demonstrating your trust in him through your giving?

3. "He makes me lie down in green pastures, he leads me beside quiet waters" verse 2). How often do you spend time in "green pastures" or beside "quiet waters" for spiritual rest and refreshment? Are you one of those sheep that God has to "make" lie down?

4. "He refreshes my soul" (verse 3a). What does it mean that God refreshes your soul? When have you recently experienced God's healing or restoration in a particular area of your life?

5. "He guides me along the right paths for his name's sake" (verse 3b). How have you seen God lead you along "right paths"? What are some ways in which he is currently leading you?

6. "Even though I walk through the darkest valley, I will fear no evil, for you are with me; your rod and your staff, they comfort me" (verse 4). How have you witnessed God comfort you during an especially "dark valley" or trying time in your life?

7. "You prepare a table before me in the presence of my enemies" (verse 5a). What does this verse say about the peace you can have in your life in spite of what is happening in the world? What kind of peace from God do you need today?

8. "You anoint my head with oil; my cup overflows" (verse 5b). What are some of the ways in which God has anointed you for service? What gifts and abilities has the Lord given to you that he desires for you use to bless others?

RESPOND | 10 MINUTES

As mentioned in the video, Jesus also described himself as a shepherd—a Good Shepherd—and said that those who choose to follow after him are his sheep. Jesus went on to explain what he does for his sheep and how he protects them from the enemy. Read through the following passage on your own and then answer the questions that follow.

> [7] Therefore Jesus said again, "Very truly I tell you, I am the gate for the sheep. [8] All who have come before me are thieves and robbers, but the sheep have not listened to them. [9] I am the gate; whoever enters through me will be saved. They will come in and go out, and find pasture. [10] The thief comes only to steal and kill and destroy; I have come that they may have life, and have it to the full. . . .
>
> [14] "I am the good shepherd; I know my sheep and my sheep know me— [15] just as the Father knows me and I know the Father—and I lay down my life for the sheep. [16] I have other sheep that are not of this sheep pen. I must bring them also. They too will listen to my voice, and there shall be one flock and one shepherd. [17] The reason my Father loves me is that I lay down my life—only to take it up again. [18] No one takes it from me, but I lay it down of my own accord. I have authority to lay it down and authority to take it up again. This command I received from my Father."
>
> **John 10:7–10, 14–18**

What promises does Jesus give to those "sheep" who choose to listen to his voice?

What does Jesus say that he is willing to do for his sheep?

What similarities do you see between Jesus' words in this passage and Psalm 23?

PRAY | 10 MINUTES

Wrap up your group's time by praying together, asking each person to pray aloud using one of the eight names/attributes for God found in Psalm 23. (Once again, these are Shepherd, Provider, Peace, Healer, Righteousness, Constant Companion, Defender, and Sanctifier). Discuss who will cover each name before you start praying. Make this prayer time focused on group praise and worship for who God is and all that he has done in each of your lives. Thank him for answering your prayers because of his lavish love for you—as members of his flock—and not because of anything you've done. Use the space below to write down any requests mentioned so that you and your group members can continue to pray about them in the week ahead.

Name   Request

personal
STUDY

In your group time this week, you explored a model for praying the names of God found in Psalm 23—one of the most well-known and best-loved passages in all the Bible. Praying the names of God and exploring aspects of his ability, nature, and power are wonderful ways to focus on the *Lord* and his qualities rather than on yourself and your own. Once again, be sure to write down your responses to the questions in the spaces provided, as you will be given a few minutes to share your insights at the start of the next session if you are doing this study with others. If you are reading *Pray First* alongside this study, first review chapter 9 in the book.

— DAY 1 —
PRAY FIRST

As you discussed in this week's group time, praying the names of God helps you to keep your focus on him. But there are other reasons why praying his names are important. In the Lord's Prayer, Jesus instructed his followers to begin praying by addressing God as their Father in heaven and by hallowing his name (see Matthew 6:9). Hallowing is simply honoring, respecting, and revering, which reinforces the third of the Ten Commandments that God gave to Moses: "You shall not take the name of the LORD your God in vain, for the LORD will not hold him guiltless who takes His name in vain" (Exodus 20:7 NKJV).

Now, it is important to remember that taking God's name in vain includes more than just swearing and cursing. *Any* time you misuse God's name, you disrespect who he is. Treating his name carelessly and trivially undermines the reverence, humility, and respect that you want to show to your Creator, Father, Lord, and Savior. On the other hand, praying the names of God is a wonderful way to hallow, honor, and worship who God is in your life.

Another important reason to pray the names of God is to exercise his power and authority over all situations that you face. Paul explains how God exalted Jesus to the highest place "and gave him the name that is above every name, that at the name of Jesus every knee should bow . . . and every tongue acknowledge that Jesus Christ is Lord, to the glory of God the Father" (Philippians 2:9–11). James adds that even the demons believe this and tremble (see 2:19). When you pray the names of God, you are connecting to the highest authority.

I. What are some names of God that you tend to use the most when addressing him in prayer? Which names do you often overlook or use infrequently?

2. What does the Third Commandment tell you about the importance of the way in which God wants you to use his name?

3. Aside from swearing, how do people often take God's name in vain? When have you regarded God's names with less respect than they deserve?

4. What is significant about God giving Jesus the "name above all names"? How does the authority of the name of Jesus impact the way you pray?

5. What kind of power and authority do you associate with the name of Jesus? When has calling on his name empowered you in a critical situation?

6. Choose one of the names of God from Psalm 23 and spend a few moments in prayer, focusing on what that name means to you and how it affects your relationship with the Lord. Why did you choose that particular name to include in your prayer?

— DAY 2 —
PRAY GOD'S WORD

Psalm 23 is not the only place you can find various names for God. The Old Testament reveals many examples of how God was known, worshiped, and honored, often based on events, places, and miraculous circumstances. As individuals discovered new facets of God's character, their revelation often included a new name for the Almighty.

As you will see below, many of these names begin with Jehovah, which is the name God revealed to Moses when calling him to lead the Israelites out of Egypt. God told Moses to explain that "The LORD, the God of your fathers—the God of Abraham, the God of Isaac and the God of Jacob—has sent me to you. This is my name forever, the name you shall call me from generation to generation" (Exodus 3:15).

Read through the list below of additional names for God, along with a verse in which each name appears. Then go through the list again, more slowly this time, and meditate on each particular attribute or aspect of God and his character. Finally, choose one of these names to focus on in prayer for the next few minutes. Use the questions included after the list to facilitate your reflection, meditation, and prayer time.

- **Jehovah: "I AM WHO I AM."** "God said to Moses, 'I AM WHO I AM. This is what you are to say to the Israelites: "I AM has sent me to you"'" (Exodus 3:14).

- **Jehovah-M'Kaddesh: The God Who Sanctifies.** "Consecrate yourselves and be holy, because I am the LORD your God. Keep my decrees and follow them. I am the LORD, who makes you holy" (Leviticus 20:7–8).

- **Jehovah-Jireh: The God Who Provides.** "Abraham looked up and there in a thicket he saw a ram caught by its horns. He went over and took the ram and sacrificed it as a burnt offering instead of his son. So Abraham called that place The LORD Will Provide. And to this day it is said, 'On the mountain of the LORD it will be provided'" (Genesis 22:13–14).

- **Jehovah-Shalom: The God of Peace.** "So Gideon built an altar to the LORD there and called it The LORD Is Peace" (Judges 6:24).

- **Jehovah-Rophe: The God Who Heals.** "If you listen carefully to the LORD your God and do what is right in his eyes, if you pay attention to his commands and keep all his decrees, I will not bring on you any of the diseases I brought on the Egyptians, for I am the LORD, who heals you" (Exodus 15:26).

- **Jehovah-Nissi: God Is Our Banner.** "Moses built an altar and called it The LORD is my Banner" (Exodus 17:15).

- **El-Shaddai: God Almighty.** "Because of the hand of the Mighty One of Jacob, because of the Shepherd, the Rock of Israel, because of your father's God, who helps you, because of the Almighty, who blesses you with blessings of the skies above" (Genesis 49:24–25).

- **Adonai: Master, Lord.** "Then King David went in and sat before the LORD, and he said: 'Who am I, Sovereign LORD, and what is my family, that you have brought me this far?'" (2 Samuel 7:18).

I. Which of these names overlap with the names and roles of God found in Psalm 23? Which of these names seem more unique and distinct?

2. What strikes you about Abraham's name for God, Jehovah-Jireh, considering his circumstances? How would you describe God's provision in this situation?

3. What do you think it means for God to be your banner, your Jehovah-Nissi? How does knowing that he goes before you victoriously affect the choices you make each day?

4. What other names and roles are included in considering God as El-Shaddai (see Genesis 49:24–25)? How do these other names reinforce his being almighty?

5. These names primarily reflect how God interacted with the people of Israel. Considering the New Testament, how many of these names apply to Jesus and to the Holy Spirit as well?

6. Based on how the Lord is working in your life right now, what name would you ascribe to him? What does this name reveal about your relationship with God in this moment?

— DAY 3 —
CULTIVATE A LIFESTYLE OF PRAYER

Read the excerpt below from chapter 9 of *Pray First*, and then answer the questions that follow.

> Throughout the Bible we find eight primary names by which God has been known to his people. While there are numerous ways to pray God's names based on examples in Scripture, one of my favorites reveals these eight different names and qualities of God—all in one concise, poetic passage.
>
> This passage comes from one of the most beloved and well-known psalms in the Bible—Psalm 23. Like me, you may have memorized it when you were growing up. This psalm is all about Jesus as the Good Shepherd and how he takes care of us . . .
>
> Praying all the names of God found in Psalm 23 carries enormous spiritual weight. Without a doubt, it's one of the most powerful ways to pray. When we pray the names of God, we focus on God and his character—not ourselves, our needs, and our requests. It may seem counterintuitive, but our needs are met as we let go of them and focus completely on who God is in all his glorious dimensions.
>
> After all, God is not answering prayers based on what you've done or who you are. He answers prayers based on who he is. And when you pray this, the outcome is clear: surely goodness and mercy will follow you all the days of your life![5]

I. Which of the eight names of God in Psalm 23 resonates with you the most? Why?

2. How has praying the names of God been powerful in your life so far? How will praying his names draw you closer to him moving forward?

3. What are some of the unique and personal names you would give to God based on your relationship with him and your journey of faith?

— DAY 4 —
TAKE INVENTORY

The eight names of God drawn from Psalm 23 are listed below. Under each one, write a one-sentence prayer reflecting the specific role of that name for you. For example, "My Good Shepherd, thank you for watching over me when I traveled for that business trip."

I. Shepherd . . .

2. Provider . . .

3. Peace . . .

4. Healer . . .

5. Righteousness . . .

6. Constant Companion . . .

7. Defender . . .

8. Sanctifier . . .

— DAY 5 —
TAKE ACTION

Now that you've explored a variety of God's names and started incorporating them into your prayers, it's time to choose one to put into action. Consider all that you've been learning in this study, both in your group and in these personal responses, and choose one name and attribute of God to demonstrate to someone else. In other words, think about how you can be the hands and feet of Jesus and become the answer to someone else's prayers.

Before your next group meeting, choose someone to serve in a specific way based on the name of God you've chosen. If possible, pick someone you know in your church, community, or neighborhood. For example, you might focus on God being the provider and provide food, money, or other resources to someone in need. If you can give your gift anonymously, it's all the better so that God gets all the credit from the recipient.

Or you could focus on God as peace by reaching out to someone you know who is going through a tough time. It's amazing how much peace you can bring to another person just by listening and by letting that person know that you care and are there to support him or her. Or you could focus on God as healer by accompanying a friend to a doctor's appointment or to receive medical treatment. You could also offer healing by listening to someone struggling with anxiety and depression and offering to pray with them if appropriate.

Ask the Holy Spirit to guide you as you choose one of God's names to activate for someone in need. Be prepared to experience a unique blessing by serving in this special way. Then take a few moments after the experience to reflect on the following questions.

I.   What was the experience like for you to minister to the person in this way?

2. How did this person respond to the act of serving and blessing on your part?

3. How does this experience help you to better understand how God relates to you?

FOR NEXT WEEK | Before you meet with your group next week, read chapter 12 in *Pray First*. (Also consider reading chapter 11 to learn about the prayers for spiritual warfare.) Read Ephesians 1:17–18 and begin thinking about what this passage says about the types of prayers that we should pray for others. Complete any of the study and reflection questions from this personal study that you weren't able to finish.

schedule

BEFORE GROUP MEETING	Read chapter 12 in *Pray First* Read the Welcome section (page 107)
GROUP MEETING	Discuss the Connect questions Watch the video teaching for session 5 Discuss the questions that follow as a group Do the closing exercise and pray (pages 107–116)
PERSONAL STUDY – DAY 1	Complete the daily study (pages 118–120)
PERSONAL STUDY – DAY 2	Complete the daily study (pages 121–123)
PERSONAL STUDY – DAY 3	Complete the daily study (pages 124–125)
PERSONAL STUDY – DAY 4	Complete the daily study (pages 126–127)
PERSONAL STUDY – DAY 5 (BEFORE WEEK 6 GROUP MEETING)	Read chapters 13–17 in *Pray First* Complete any unfinished personal studies (pages 128–129)

my prayer for you

No matter where you are in life or in your journey of faith, you can experience the fullness of what God wants to give you.

CHRIS HODGES

WELCOME | READ ON YOUR OWN

How often have you told someone you would pray for them and then struggled to know exactly *what* to pray? Beyond a specific request or need of which you are aware, it can be difficult to know how to pray outside of using vague and general terms. The challenge can be even greater when you feel led to pray for those whom you do not know well.

Fortunately, the apostle Paul gives us a great model for praying for others (as well as ourselves) in a letter he wrote to believers in the early church at Ephesus. You may recall that Paul was a church planter, and many of the books in the New Testament are actually letters that he wrote to those new churches. While most of these letters— or epistles, as they're often called—provide instruction, doctrine, and encouragement, the one we now call the book of Ephesians contains a model prayer that Paul prayed for all these new believers.

God makes it clear throughout his Word that there is a path of life we can follow that bears fruit, shines light, and leads to fulfillment. Paul's prayer basically categorizes this path of life into four areas, each of which reflects the spiritual journey we experience as we mature in our faith. Knowing these four areas, and pursuing them, will help us make sense of our lives and enjoy them to the fullest. It will also help us to know what to pray for others!

CONNECT | 15 MINUTES

Get the session started by choosing one of the following questions to discuss as a group:

- What is a key insight or takeaway from last week's personal study that you would like to share with the group?

  — or —

- How often do you ask other people to pray for you? What do you usually *hope* that they will pray for you?

WATCH | 20 MINUTES

Now watch the video for this session. As you go through the material, use the following outline to record any thoughts or concepts that stand out to you.

I. The picture that God has for our lives

    A. In Psalm 92:13, we read that "those who are planted in the house of the Lord shall flourish in the courts of our God" (NKJV). God doesn't want us just to *survive* but to *flourish.*

    B. Like Death Valley, there are seeds of potential within all of us that are just waiting to be watered. These seeds will grow when we take the steps that God wants us to take.

    C. In Psalm 16:11, we read that God will show us "the path of life; in Your presence is fullness of joy; at Your right hand are pleasures forevermore" (NKJV). When we follow the path of life that God sets for us, it leads to fullness and joy.

II. The pathway of life in Paul's prayer for his churches

  A. Pray that you may know God better

    1. "I keep asking that the God of our Lord Jesus Christ . . . give you the Spirit of wisdom and revelation, so that you may know him better" (Ephesians 1:17). The word that Paul uses for *know* in the Greek refers not to mental knowledge but to intimate knowledge.

    2. Jesus was never looking for some type of religious following. He was always looking for a relationship. He wants to have an intimate relationship with us.

    3. Once we are in a close relationship with God, it empowers the next three steps in the spiritual journey. In fact, we can't do the next steps without this one.

B. Pray to overcome the issues that hold you back

    1. "I pray that the eyes of your heart may be enlightened" (verse 18a). We all look through the "eyes" of our heart. We look at everything through the lens of what has happened to us in the past, so we all see things differently based on what has happened to us in our lives.

    2. All of us have something that holds us back from being the "better" version of ourselves—from moving to the next place in our spiritual journey that God desires for us. God's plan is actually for us to deal with these issues.

    3. We go to God for forgiveness, but we go to God's people for healing. The power is found in the confession and the honesty and the transparency. God wants us to be free.

C. Pray for God to reveal your real purpose in life

    1. "In order that you may know the hope to which he has called you" (verse 18b). We pray that God will help us to live in such a way that we discover our true life's purpose.

    2. Much of the New Testament is about the spiritual gifts, calling, and purpose that we have in the body of Christ as members of the family of God.

    3. Paul states in Romans 12:6 that we have different gifts according to the grace give to each of us. The Greek word for grace in this verse is *charis,* and it refers to a divine enablement.

D. Pray for God to use you to make a difference

    1. "The riches of his glorious inheritance in his holy people" (Ephesians 1:18c). Our real purpose in life isn't our careers, paying bills and surviving, or even just enjoying life. Our whole purpose in life is to make an eternal difference in the lives of others.

    2. Jesus said, "I have told you this so that my joy may be in you and that your joy may be complete" (John 15:11). Serving others helps us by providing joy and fulfillment in our lives.

    3. If we want to find our purpose, we are going to need to get involved in our local church. We find our purpose when we are around the other members of the body of Christ.

DISCUSS | 35 MINUTES

Discuss what you just watched by answering the following questions as time allows.

I. The first part of Paul's prayer is: "I keep asking that the God of our Lord Jesus Christ . . . may give you the Spirit of wisdom and revelation, so that you may know him better" (Ephesians 1:17). What are some of the ways in which you would like to get to know God better?

2. The second part of Paul's prayer is: "I pray that the eyes of your heart may be enlightened" (verse 18a). What might be some things that you have been seeing with the "eyes of your heart"? How do you think this vision and perspective have impacted your prayer life?

3. The third part of Paul's prayer is: "[I pray] that you make know the hope to which he has called you" (verse 18b). What has God revealed to you about your purpose in life so far? Do you feel as though you have a clear idea about "the hope to which he has called you"?

4. The final part of Paul's prayer is: "[I pray that you may know] the riches of his glorious inheritance in his holy people" (verse 18c). What difference would you most like to make in the lives of those around you? What do you want your spiritual legacy to be?

5. Which of these four areas of prayer seems especially significant to you right now? Why?

6. In James 5:16 we read, "Confess your sins to each other and pray for each other so that you may be healed." Based on your experience, do you agree that we go to God for forgiveness but to God's people for healing? Why or why not?

7. What is one spiritual gift that you believe you have or that you have been told by others that you have? How have you used this gift to serve others?

8. What stands out or resonates in this prayer compared to the other prayer models explored in previous sessions? Why?

RESPOND | 10 MINUTES

In this week's teaching, you looked at two verses from the book of Psalms that describe the kind of life that God wants all of his children to have. Take a few moments to read through these verses in context on your own and then answer the questions that follow.

> ¹² The righteous will flourish like a palm tree,
>   they will grow like a cedar of Lebanon;
> ¹³ planted in the house of the Lᴏʀᴅ,
>   they will flourish in the courts of our God.
> ¹⁴ They will still bear fruit in old age,
>   they will stay fresh and green,
> ¹⁵ proclaiming, "The Lᴏʀᴅ is upright;
>   he is my Rock, and there is no wickedness in him."
>
> **Psalm 92:12–15**

> ⁷ I will praise the Lᴏʀᴅ, who counsels me;
>   even at night my heart instructs me.
> ⁸ I keep my eyes always on the Lᴏʀᴅ.
>   With him at my right hand, I will not be shaken.
> ⁹ Therefore my heart is glad and my tongue rejoices;
>   my body also will rest secure,
> ¹⁰ because you will not abandon me to the realm of the dead,
>   nor will you let your faithful one see decay.
> ¹¹ You make known to me the path of life;
>   you will fill me with joy in your presence,
>   with eternal pleasures at your right hand.
>
> **Psalm 16:7–11**

How is the life of a righteous person described in Psalm 92:12–15?

For what does the writer praise the Lord in Psalm 16:7–11?

What is required on your part to walk "the path of life" that God has revealed?

PRAY | 10 MINUTES

As you conclude this session, go around the room and share which of these four areas—knowing God better, overcoming issues, discovering purpose, making a difference—you would like others to pray for you. You can be personal and specific or just indicate the general category. Then spend a few minutes praying for each other and any other needs or requests as the Holy Spirit leads. Thank God for the ways in which he helps you discover your next steps on your spiritual journey. Use the space below to write down any requests mentioned so that you and your group members can continue to pray about them in the week ahead.

Name   Request

personal
STUDY

This week, you discussed a prayer that Paul prayed for a congregation located in Ephesus. You saw that Paul prayed that the believers would know God better, overcome issues that held them back, understand God's purpose for their lives, and be used by God to make a difference. As you keep these four areas from Paul's prayer in mind, try to become more aware this week of how you can pray for those around you. Continue reflecting on where you see yourself on your spiritual journey and what next steps the Holy Spirit may be calling you to take. Again, write down your responses to the questions in the spaces provided, as you will be given a few minutes to share your insights at the start of the next session if you are doing this study with others. If you are reading *Pray First* alongside this study, first review chapter 12 in the book.

— DAY 1 —
PRAY FIRST

Paul begins his prayer for the believers in Ephesus by asking God to give them "the Spirit of wisdom and revelation" so that they might "know him better" (Ephesians 1:16). Placing this request at the beginning of his prayer emphasizes its importance. Clearly, Paul wanted these followers of Jesus to know God intimately and to grow in their knowledge of him.

This same kind of deep "knowing" is also fundamental to your spiritual growth. Your relationship with God sets the foundation for all the other progressive stages. Knowing him is an ongoing process over a lifetime, not a one-time memorization of facts or theology. No matter your circumstances or season of life, your relationship with God keeps you anchored.

As discussed in this week's group time, knowing God the way that Paul describes here is not necessarily knowledge in the sense of facts and information. You can know a lot about someone—through other people, secondhand information, historical records, and social media—without having a firsthand relationship that allows you to know that individually personally. This kind of knowledge is often distant, detached, and objective.

Instead of merely factual knowledge, Paul is referring to a personal, experiential, and intimate relationship with God. The Greek word he uses is *ginosko,* which was heavily influenced by the Hebrew word *yada,* which we find in the Old Testament as a polite euphemism for the way a husband and wife know one another (see, for example, Genesis 4:1). This kind of intense closeness begins when you enter into a spiritual relationship with God through his Son, Jesus, and the power of the Holy Spirit dwelling within you.

Everything starts with knowing God. Knowing God is paramount to all the other aspects of your spiritual journey. In fact, you can't take the next three steps of the spiritual journey in Paul's prayer without this first one. Jesus reinforced this truth in the following passage:

> [21] "Not everyone who says to me, 'Lord, Lord,' will enter the kingdom of heaven, but only the one who does the will of my Father who is in heaven. [22] Many will say to me on that day, 'Lord, Lord, did we not prophesy in your name and in your name drive out demons and in your name perform many miracles?' [23] Then I will tell them plainly, 'I never knew you. Away from me, you evildoers!'"
>
> **Matthew 7:21–23**

Clearly, *knowing* God should be your priority—not merely *learning* about him or *serving* others in his name. You do this by spending time with him, praising and worshiping him, talking with and listening to him. The more you get to know him, the more you will want to know him.

1. How do you respond to this statement that you just read from Jesus? What is surprising (and even shocking) in his words?

2. What stands out to you in the warning Jesus gives about those who will claim to know him without doing the will of his Father?

3. Based on the warning Christ gives, how can you make sure that you are not just performing acts for God but actually knowing him?

4. Think about some friends you know really well. How does relating to them over time allow you to experience more than just factual knowledge about them?

5. Similarly, how has your knowledge of God developed or changed over time? What do you know about him now that you didn't when you started out in your relationship with him?

6. What's one aspect of God's character you would like to know more about? What next step can you take to discover more about this aspect of his nature?

— DAY 2 —
PRAY GOD'S WORD

One request that Paul makes in his prayer is that we would find freedom through the power of Jesus Christ: "I pray that the eyes of your heart may be enlightened in order that you may know the hope to which he has called you" (Ephesians 1:18). Paul wants us to have *spiritual clarity*, using the "eyes of our hearts," so we can see God's purposes and live them out.

However, to have such clarity, our heart needs to be clean and clear. Our heart is a filter for how we see things in life and is impacted by our hurts, wounds, trials, and triumphs. God's Word instructs, "Keep your heart with all diligence, for out of it spring the issues of life" (Proverbs 4:23 NKJV). To keep our hearts clear, we need to remove the pollution of sin that will cloud our spiritual vision. We do this through confession to God and his people.

One of the greatest prayers of confession is found in Psalm 51. King David composed this psalm after he was confronted by the prophet Nathan about his adulterous affair with Bathsheba and his deceptive plan that resulted in her husband's death. This psalm was about clearing his vision by purifying his heart. You can likewise use this psalm as a means to clarify your own "heart lens" so that you can clearly see all that God has for you.

Read through this psalm slowly and think of areas in your life you that need to confess to the Lord. Make the words your own as you seek his grace to restore your relationship with him. Use the questions that follow to make this psalm your own prayer of repentance.

> [1] Have mercy on me, O God,
>   according to your unfailing love;
> according to your great compassion
>   blot out my transgressions.
> [2] Wash away all my iniquity
>   and cleanse me from my sin.

> ³ For I know my transgressions,
>   and my sin is always before me.
> ⁴ Against you, you only, have I sinned
>   and done what is evil in your sight;
> so you are right in your verdict
>   and justified when you judge. . . .
>
> ¹⁰ Create in me a pure heart, O God,
>   and renew a steadfast spirit within me.
> ¹¹ Do not cast me from your presence
>   or take your Holy Spirit from me.
> ¹² Restore to me the joy of your salvation
>   and grant me a willing spirit, to sustain me.
>
> **Psalm 51:1-4, 10-12**

1. According to the psalmist, what is the source of God's mercy?

2. What transgressions come to mind that may be hindering your ability to see clearly?

3. How does God renew a steadfast spirit within you when you confess your sins to him?

4. What does it mean to you to be "restored to the joy of your salvation"?

5. How does having a "willing spirit" sustain you on your spiritual journey?

6. What else do you still need to confess to restore your relationship with the Lord?

— DAY 3 —
CULTIVATE A LIFESTYLE OF PRAYER

Read the excerpt below from chapter 12 of *Pray First*, and then answer the questions that follow.

> Once you've found freedom and experienced victory over your big issues, then you can discover your purpose and live out the calling God has placed on your life. You can't discover purpose if you haven't found freedom.
>
> Many people don't see their God-given purpose because they're limited by the cloudy lens they're using. When you see clearly and find your calling, it brings hope to your life. Other than the day you were born, the two most important days in your life are the day you are born again and the day you figure out why you were born. Without clarity, you miss out on the journey of joy that God wants to take you on.
>
> Everyone has God-given gifts that are unique to you and your journey. God's Word says, "We have different gifts, according to the grace given to each of us" (Romans 12:6). The original Greek word here for "gifts," or literally "grace gifts," is *charis*—the same root from which we get the words charisma and charismatic. "God has given each of you a gift from his great variety of spiritual gifts. Use them well to serve one another" (1 Peter 4:10 NLT). . . .
>
> God has given all of us different gifts—but we have to know what they are in order to use them. "Now about the gifts of the Spirit, brothers and sisters, I do not want you to be uninformed" (1 Corinthians 12:1). Too many people are ignorant of their *charis*-abilities. This has to change if you want to live the full, abundant life God has for you![6]

I. Do you agree that you can't discover your God-given purpose without first experiencing the freedom you have in Christ? Why or why not?

2. Where are you presently in the process of discovering and living out of your divine purpose? What has helped clarify your understanding of your purpose?

3. How does knowing and living out your purpose enable you to have a greater impact for God's kingdom?

— DAY 4 —
TAKE INVENTORY

Review the four key areas in Paul's prayer for the Ephesians that are listed below. Reflect on your own journey with God and briefly describe your personal experience for each area.

I. Pray that you may know God better

2. Pray to overcome the issues that hold you back

3. Pray for God to reveal your real purpose in life

4. Pray for God to use you to make a difference

— DAY 5 —
TAKE ACTION

As discussed in this week's group time, you go to God for *forgiveness*, but you go to God's people for *healing* (see James 5:16). This process may sound scary—even intimidating and overwhelming—but if you are serious about overcoming the issues that hold you back, you need to be in a community with other followers of Jesus where you can be known, do life together, and encourage one another to grow in your faith.

God's Word says, "Let us think of ways to motivate one another to acts of love and good works. And let us not neglect our meeting together, as some people do, but encourage one another, especially now that the day of his return is drawing near" (Hebrews 10:24–25 NLT). Confession with other believers requires vulnerability and trust. But as soon as you confess your faults one to another and pray for one another, the Bible promises healing.

Before your final group meeting, choose to meet with a believer you know and trust, either from your group, your church, or elsewhere. Spend time in prayer before you meet with that person and unburden your heart before the Lord. Ask the person to listen and pray with you after you have shared and confessed all that's been obscuring your spiritual vision. If the person so desires, be willing to return the favor as he or she confesses to you.

Take a few moments after your time together to reflect on the following questions.

1.   What was the hardest part of making this confession to the other person?

2. What impact did the experience have on you in terms of unburdening your heart?

3. What would you need to do to make this practice a regular part of your spiritual journey?

FOR NEXT WEEK | Before you meet with your group next week, read chapters 13–17 in *Pray First.* Begin thinking about how you view the spiritual practice of fasting found in the Bible and the questions you have about it. Go back and complete any of the study and reflection questions from this personal study that you weren't able to finish.

schedule

WEEK 6

BEFORE GROUP MEETING	Read chapters 13–17 in *Pray First* Read the Welcome section (page 132)
GROUP MEETING	Discuss the Connect questions Watch the video teaching for session 6 Discuss the questions that follow as a group Do the closing exercise and pray (pages 132–140)
PERSONAL STUDY – DAY 1	Complete the daily study (pages 142–143)
PERSONAL STUDY – DAY 2	Complete the daily study (pages 144–146)
PERSONAL STUDY – DAY 3	Complete the daily study (pages 147–148)
PERSONAL STUDY – DAY 4	Complete the daily study (pages 149)
PERSONAL STUDY – DAY 5	Finish the final session (pages 150–151). Connect with your group about the next study that you want to go through together.

prayer and fasting

Fasting takes prayer to another level in our faith and effectiveness in the prayers we pray.

CHRIS HODGES

WELCOME | READ ON YOUR OWN

What comes to mind when you hear the word *fasting*? Perhaps you view it as a hard-core spiritual discipline for the "elite"—the pastors, missionaries, and spiritual leaders of the world. Or maybe you view fasting as an outdated practice that is no longer relevant for believers today. You might even believe fasting is primarily a weight-loss tool or health practice!

At its core, however, fasting is a spiritual practice for anyone seeking more of God. Fasting can take your prayers to another level. The act of fasting—choosing for a set period to abstain from food, sugar, social media, music, or anything else that consumes energy and takes your attention away from God—can help you fully experience your freedom in Christ.

In contrast to the message in our society to *consume,* fasting is a practice in which you seek to *deny* what your flesh craves for a time. When you suppress those cravings and force your body to yield to your spirit, you create space for drawing closer to God. When your will is aligned with his own, you have full access to his unlimited power through the Holy Spirit, including the power to overcome any areas that are holding you back in your faith.

Simply put, fasting is easier than you think and more powerful than you might realize. So, as we conclude the *Pray First* study, we will take a closer look at this important biblical practice.

CONNECT | 15 MINUTES

Get the session started by choosing one of the following questions to discuss as a group:

- What is a key insight or takeaway from last week's personal study that you would like to share with the group?

  — or —

- Other than food, what is something to which you often turn for a pleasurable distraction? Watching TV? Social media? Sports? Shopping? Something else?

WATCH | 20 MINUTES

Now watch the video for this session. As you go through the material, use the following outline to record any thoughts or concepts that stand out to you.

I. The importance of fasting in connection to prayer

A. In Matthew 17:14–20, we read that Jesus' disciples were unable to bring healing to a demon-possessed boy. So the father brought the child to Jesus and asked him for healing.

B. Jesus identified two reasons why the disciples could not drive the demon out of the boy—they were "unbelieving and perverse" (verse 17).

1. **Unbelieving:** *not connected to God.* In other words, their faith was weak.

2. **Perverse:** *too connected to the world.* The disciples were being influenced by the world.

C. Jesus provides the solution to the problem: "this kind does not go out except by prayer and fasting" (verse 21 NKJV). Prayer and fasting can be defined in this way:

    1. Prayer connects us to God.

    2. Fasting disconnects us from the world.

II. Three principles for prayer and fasting

  A. Set your objective

    1. Decide why you are fasting. Have a focus in mind before you begin a fast. Set specific goals and objectives that line up with God's priorities.

    2. Know what you are believing God to provide when you come to him in prayer and fasting. Share this objective with others and make your request public.

B. Decide what type of fast you will do

1. Complete fast: A fast in which you are simply drinking liquids. (Be sure to always get medical supervision and just use good sense before you begin a complete fast.)

2. Selective fast: A fast in which you remove certain food types or food groups from your diet. One example is the Daniel Fast, in which you don't eat meat, sweets, or bread.

3. Partial fast: A fast in which you pick certain meals in the day to skip, such as breakfast or lunch. Replace the time you would have spent eating by spending time with God.

4. Soul fast: A fast in which you choose to not engage in certain things that feed your mind, will, or emotions, such as abstaining from social media. You get away from "life as usual" and instead choose to fix your mind on the things of the Lord.

C. Expect results

1. **Healing:** When you fast and pray, God will bring healing to the broken things in your life—your body, relationships, mind, emotions, and other areas.

2. **Holiness:** When you fast and pray, God will show you areas that have been grieving him so you can change those things and grow closer to him.

3. **Help:** When you fast and pray, God's favor and blessing will be on your life.

DISCUSS | 35 MINUTES

Discuss what you just watched by answering the following questions as time allows.

1. What are some inaccuracies or misperceptions you have held about fasting? How have these impacted your openness to fasting as a spiritual practice?

2. Jesus identified two reasons in Matthew 17:17 why the disciples couldn't drive out the demon: they were "unbelieving and perverse." How would you define each of these terms?

3. Think about the definition of prayer and fasting given during the teaching. How does fasting provide the solution to the problem of being "unbelieving and perverse"?

4. The first principle when it comes to fasting is to *set your objective.* What are you believing today for God to provide in your life? What are some objectives you could set for fasting?

5. The second principle of fasting is to *decide what type of fast your will do.* What type of fast covered in this week's teaching most appeals to you? Why that particular fast?

6. The third principle of fasting is to *expect results.* What three things can you expect God to do in your life when you fast and pray? Which do you need the most in your life right now?

7. How has your understanding of the relationship between prayer and fasting changed in light of this week's teaching?

8. How do you feel led to incorporate fasting into your life moving forward? What benefits do you hope to gain from adding fasting to your prayer life?

RESPOND | 10 MINUTES

The Bible states that Jesus "called his twelve disciples to him and gave them authority to drive out impure spirits and to heal every disease and sickness" (Matthew 10:1). However, as you saw in this week's teaching, those same disciples were unable to draw a demon out of one particular boy. Read the following passage on your own and answer the questions that follow.

> [14] And when they had come to the multitude, a man came to Him, kneeling down to Him and saying, [15] "Lord, have mercy on my son, for he is an epileptic and suffers severely; for he often falls into the fire and often into the water. [16] So I brought him to Your disciples, but they could not cure him."
>
> [17] Then Jesus answered and said, "O faithless and perverse generation, how long shall I be with you? How long shall I bear with you? Bring him here to Me." [18] And Jesus rebuked the demon, and it came out of him; and the child was cured from that very hour.
>
> [19] Then the disciples came to Jesus privately and said, "Why could we not cast it out?"
>
> [20] So Jesus said to them, "Because of your unbelief; for assuredly, I say to you, if you have faith as a mustard seed, you will say to this mountain, 'Move from here to there,' and it will move; and nothing will be impossible for you. [21] However, this kind does not go out except by prayer and fasting."
>
> **Matthew 17:14–21** NKJV

How would you explain Jesus' reaction to the father after hearing this week's teaching?

What does Jesus say to the disciples to encourage them to have faith in God?

Why do you thinking fasting allows us to tap into more of God's unlimited power?

PRAY | 10 MINUTES

As you conclude this last session, go around the group and share one important take-away that you have learned about prayer during the course of this study. Share any personal prayer requests that you would like the others to pray about, both now and after this final session. Thank God for all that he has shown you, taught you, and given you through this small-group study. Ask for his continued blessings on each of you as the group completes this time together. Finally, use the space below to write down any requests mentioned so that you and your group members can continue to pray about them in the weeks ahead.

Name   Request

personal
STUDY

In your final group time this week, you discussed the connection between prayer and fasting and saw how prayer *connects* you with God while fasting *disconnects* you from the world. You looked at three principles to keep in mind when planning a fast and reviewed some different types of fasts. In this final personal study, you will continue exploring the benefits of fasting with prayer and start to plan out what type of fast you would like to engage in to enhance your intimacy and connection with God. If you are reading *Pray First* alongside this study, first review chapters 13–17 in the book. At the end of this study, you will be asked to keep in touch with group members as you continue to encourage and uphold one another in prayer. This is a great way to practice what you've learned about prayer as you grow in your faith.

— DAY 1 —
PRAY FIRST

Begin this final time of personal study by reviewing your ideas about prayer. Focus on what is new, different, or more mature in your view of prayer as compared to when you first started this study. Write down all the things that you especially appreciate from your time with the group, from reading the *Pray First* book, and from completing this study. Feel free to make your own list or use the following prompts to get you started.

I.   One significant way that my view of prayer has changed is . . .

2.   This is what I have done to make prayer a daily priority in my life . . .

3.   This is what I have done to find a place and have a plan for prayer . . .

4. I have witnessed the power of God in this way since beginning this study . . .

5. The prayer model that I have found to be the most effective is . . .

6. I feel that I have grown closer to the Father, Son, and Holy Spirit in this way . . .

— DAY 2 —
PRAY GOD'S WORD

The focus of this week's group time was on prayer and fasting. Once you have decided to fast, you need to choose what type you will do and for what length of time. You might want to fast with others as part of a focused effort in your small group, church, or Bible study. But don't feel any pressure to do what others are doing—your fast is solely between you and the Lord. Jesus emphasized the intimacy of your personal choice to fast in this way:

> [16] "When you fast, do not look somber as the hypocrites do, for they disfigure their faces to show men they are fasting. I tell you the truth, they have received their reward in full. [17] But when you fast, put oil on your head and wash your face, [18] so that it will not be obvious to men that you are fasting, but only to your Father, who is unseen; and your Father, who sees what is done in secret, will reward you."
>
> **Matthew 6:16–18**

Remember, you shouldn't attempt to fast if you have any medical or dietary reasons that prohibit you from abstaining from food. Just use plain old common sense about what you can do within your health restrictions and lifestyle limitations. The goal is not to lose weight or even to experience the health benefits that accompany fasting. Your goal is to experience the "spirit of fasting," which can only happen in your spirit as you focus on knowing God.

Ultimately, fasting is a matter of your heart, not your diet. It is not about food as much as it is about removing certain things from your life so you can draw closer to God. Sometimes the fast itself can become a distraction, especially if you're new to this practice. Fasting is not about gritting yourself through a discipline in order to say you accomplished it. Rather, it is about surrendering your appetites to God in order to feast on more of him. As you consider adding a fast to your prayer practice, use the following questions to aid in your decision.

I. Why do you think Jesus told his followers to be discrete when they fasted? How does letting everyone know that you are fasting defeat the purpose?

2. What type of fast are you drawn to practicing? How long will the fast you are planning last?

3. What health or dietary concerns do you have about fasts involving food? When can you consult your doctor or other health professional to discuss these concerns?

4. What does it mean to you that fasting is a matter of your heart and not your diet? What do you personally see as the primary benefit of fasting?

5. If you decide to practice a soul fast, what item (or items) in your life would you give up? Why would you choose this particular thing to give up?

6. Prayer connects us with God. Fasting disconnects us with the world. Given this, what are you hoping to gain at the end of this time of prayer and fasting?

— DAY 3 —
CULTIVATE A LIFESTYLE OF PRAYER

Read the excerpt below from chapter 13 of *Pray First*, and then answer the questions that follow.

Fasting is mentioned in the Bible not a couple times, not a dozen times, but more than seventy times! In fact, Jesus said that his people would need to fast to remain connected to him in his absence, once he had left earth and returned to heaven: "Then John's disciples came and asked him, 'How is it that we and the Pharisees fast often, but your disciples do not *fast*?' Jesus answered, 'How can the guests of the bridegroom mourn while he is with them? The time will come when the bridegroom will be taken from them; *then they will fast*'" (Matthew 9:14–15, emphasis added).

Fasting was a vital part of life in the New Testament church, in both big decisions and daily moments. "While they were worshiping the Lord and *fasting*, the Holy Spirit said, 'Set apart for me Barnabas and Saul for the work to which I have called them.' So after they had *fasted and prayed*, they placed their hands on them and sent them off" (Acts 13:2–3, emphasis added). We also find that the apostle Paul fasted as a regular discipline: ". . . in weariness and toil, in sleeplessness often, in hunger and thirst, in fastings often" (2 Corinthians 11:27 NKJV). . . .

If you're unable to fast from food for whatever reason, don't assume that fasting is irrelevant to your faith. Because there are plenty of other pleasures and distractions that anyone desiring to connect to God can give up—secular music and movies, video games, social media, and basically any pastime used to provide escape, comfort, pleasure, and relief. Here's what you will discover if you haven't already: Whatever you starve *dies*. Whatever you feed *thrives*.[7]

I. Using a scale from 1 to 10, with 1 being "not much" and 10 being "extremely," how relevant do you consider fasting to your personal relationship with God? Why?

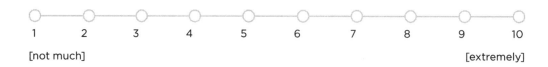

1   2   3   4   5   6   7   8   9   10

[not much]   [extremely]

2. Do you agree that whatever you starve *dies* and whatever you feed *thrives*? When have you experienced this in your journey of faith?

3. What non-food items—shopping, social media, video gaming, TV viewing, news watching, to name a few—would be hardest for you to give up during a soul fast? How do you currently rely on these items for comfort, distraction, and escape?

— DAY 4 —
TAKE INVENTORY

Complete the chart below to assess how each of the four fasts covered in this week's group time might work for you.

Kind of fast	Items given up	Duration	Goal/benefit
Complete fast			
Selective fast			
Partial fast			
Soul fast			

— DAY 5 —
TAKE ACTION

Healthy relationships and fellowship with other believers are essential for growing in your faith. With this truth in mind, take a few moments today to think back on each of your group's sessions and how each contributed to your experience. Remember each group member and consider how he or she contributed to your overall enjoyment of the group. Use the following questions to help bring closure to this study, even as you carry your experience with you and continue to improve both the quality and quantity of your prayer time.

1. What are some of the specific moments, people, and words from your group's meetings for which you're particularly thankful?

2. What surprised you the most about your group experience after completing this study? What disappointed you?

3. What will you carry with you now that your group has concluded this study?

4. Which group member or members had the greatest impact on your experience with this study? How did they bless you with their words, questions, prayers, and actions?

NEXT STEPS | Pray for each member of your group and thank God for how he is using him or her to bless others. Choose one or two other group members and send them a text, email, or call in the upcoming week to let them know that you are praying for them. When you connect, ask who they chose to reach out to from your group. Make sure that everyone in your group hears from someone else. If the group wants to continue meeting, make a plan for your next study. If the group disbands, continue checking in and asking how you can pray for them.

LEADER'S GUIDE

Thank you for your willingness to lead your group through this study! What you have chosen to do is valuable and will make a great difference in the lives of others. The rewards of being a leader are different from those of participating, and we hope that as you lead you will find your own journey with God and with prayer deepened by this experience.

Pray First is a six-session Bible study built around video content and small-group interaction. As the group leader, imagine yourself as the host of a party. Your job is to take care of your guests by managing the details so that when your guests arrive, they can focus on one another and on the interaction around the topic for that session.

Your role as the group leader is not to answer all the questions or reteach the content—the video, book, and study guide will do most of that work. Your job is to guide the experience and cultivate your small group into a connected and engaged community. This will make it a place for members to process, question, and reflect—not necessarily receive more instruction.

There are several elements in this leader's guide that will help you as you structure your study and reflection time, so be sure to follow along and take advantage of each one.

BEFORE YOU BEGIN

Before your first meeting, make sure the group members have a copy of this study guide. Alternately, you can hand out the study guides at your first meeting and give the members some time to look over the material and ask any preliminary questions. Also make sure they are aware that they have access to the streaming videos at any time by following the instructions printed on the inside front cover. During your first meeting, ask the members to provide their name, phone number, and email address so you can keep in touch with them.

Generally, the ideal size for a group is eight to ten people, which will ensure that everyone has enough time to participate in discussions. If you have more people, break up the main group into smaller subgroups. Encourage those who show up at the first meeting to commit to attending for the duration of the study, as this will help the group members get to know one another, create stability for the group, learn how to pray with one another, and help you know how to best prepare to lead them through the material.

Each of the sessions begins with an opening reflection in the Welcome section. The questions that follow in the Connect section serve as an icebreaker to get the group members thinking about the topic. Some people may want to tell a long story in response to one of these questions, but the goal is to keep the answers brief. Ideally, you want everyone in the group to get a chance to answer, so try to keep the responses to a minute or less. If you have talkative group members, say up front that everyone needs to limit their answer to one minute.

Give the group members a chance to answer, but also tell them to feel free to pass if they wish. With the rest of the study, it's generally not a good idea to have everyone answer every question—a free-flowing discussion is more desirable. But with the opening icebreaker questions, you can go around the circle. Encourage shy people to share, but don't force them.

At your first meeting, let the group members know that each session contains a personal study section they can use to continue to engage with the content until the next meeting. While this is optional, it will help them cement the concepts presented during the group study time. Let them know that if they choose to do so, they can watch the video for the next session by accessing the streaming code found on the inside front cover of their study guides. Invite them to bring any questions and insights to your next meeting, especially if they had a breakthrough moment or didn't understand something.

PREPARATION FOR EACH SESSION

As the leader, there are a few things you should do to prepare for each meeting:

- **Read through the session.** This will help you become more familiar with the content and know how to structure the discussion times.

- **Decide how the videos will be used.** Determine whether you want the members to watch the videos ahead of time (again, via the streaming access code found on the inside front cover) or together as a group.

- **Decide which questions you want to discuss.** Based on the length of your group discussions, you may not be able to get through all the questions. So look over the recommendations for the suggested and additional questions in each session and choose which ones you definitely want to cover.

- **Be familiar with the questions you want to discuss.** When the group meets you'll be watching the clock, so make sure you are familiar with the questions that you have selected. In this way, you will ensure that you have the material more deeply in your mind than do your group members.

- **Pray for your group.** Pray for your group members and ask God to lead them as they study his Word and explore these concepts on prayer.

In many cases, there will be no one "right" answer to the question. Answers will vary, especially when the group members are being asked to share their personal experiences.

STRUCTURING THE DISCUSSION TIME

You will need to determine with your group how long you want to meet so you can plan your time accordingly. Suggested times for each section have been provided in this study guide, and if you adhere to these times, your group will meet for ninety minutes, as noted below. If you want to meet for two hours, follow the times given in the right-hand column:

Section	90 Minutes	120 Minutes
CONNECT (discuss one or more of the opening questions for the session)	15 minutes	20 minutes
WATCH (watch the teaching material together and take notes)	20 minutes	20 minutes
DISCUSS (discuss the study questions you selected ahead of time)	35 minutes	50 minutes
RESPOND (do the closing personal activity)	10 minutes	15 minutes
PRAY (pray together and dismiss)	10 minutes	15 minutes

As the group leader, it is up to you to keep track of the time and keep things on schedule. You might want to set a timer for each segment so both you and the group members know when your time is up. (There are some good phone apps for timers that play a gentle chime or other pleasant sound instead of a disruptive noise.)

Don't be concerned if the group members are quiet or slow to share. People are often quiet when they are pulling together their ideas, and this might be a new experience for them. Just ask a question and let it hang in the air until someone shares. You can then say, "Thank you. What about others? What came to you when you watched that portion of the teaching?"

GROUP DYNAMICS

Leading a group through *Pray First* will prove to be highly rewarding both to you and your group members. But you still may encounter challenges along the way! Discussions can get off track. Group members may not be sensitive to the needs and ideas of others. Some might worry that they will be expected to talk about matters that make them feel awkward. Others may express comments that result in disagreements. To help ease this strain on you and the group, consider the following ground rules:

- When someone raises a question or comment that is off the main topic, suggest that you deal with it another time, or, if you feel led to go in that direction, let the group know you will be spending some time discussing it.

- If someone asks a question that you don't know how to answer, admit it and move on. At your discretion, feel free to invite group members to comment on questions that call for personal experience.

- If you find one or two people are dominating the discussion time, direct a few questions to others in the group. Outside the main group time, ask the more dominating members to help you draw out the quieter ones. Work to make them a part of the solution instead of part of the problem.

- When a disagreement occurs, encourage the group members to process the matter in love. Encourage those on opposite sides to restate what they heard the other side say about the matter, and then invite each side to evaluate whether that perception is accurate. Lead the group in examining other Scriptures related to the topic and look for common ground.

When any of these issues arise, encourage your group members to follow these words from Scripture: "Love one another" (John 13:34), "If it is possible, as far as it depends on you, live at peace with everyone" (Romans 12:18), "Whatever is true . . . noble . . . right . . . if anything is excellent or praiseworthy—think about such things" (Philippians 4:8), and, "Be quick to listen, slow to speak and slow to become angry" (James 1:19). This will make your group time more rewarding and beneficial for everyone who attends.

Thank you again for leading your group. You are making a difference in your group members' lives and having an impact on their journey toward learning how to *pray first*.

ENDNOTES

1. Chris Hodges, *Pray First* (Nashville, TN: Nelson Books, 2023), xiv–xv.
2. *Merriam-Webster*, s.v. "hallow," https://www.merriam-webster.com/dictionary/hallow.
3. Hodges, *Pray First*, 76–78.
4. Hodges, *Pray First*, 110.
5. Hodges, *Pray First*, 122, 136.
6. Hodges, *Pray First*, 173–175.
7. Hodges, *Pray First*, 188–190.

COMPANION BOOK TO ENRICH YOUR STUDY EXPERIENCE

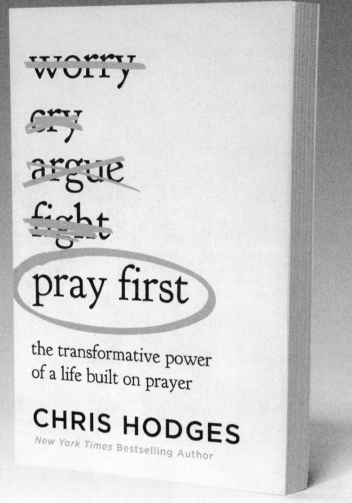

ISBN 9781400221295

Available wherever books are sold

NELSON BOOKS

An Imprint of Thomas Nelson

In this six-session video Bible study and book, Chris Hodges examines the dilemma facing all Christians today: how can we influence a world that rejects everything we believe while still standing for God's truth? Chris looks at the lives of Daniel and Jesus, showing how we can stand for our biblical beliefs without alienating those we want to reach. The goal is never about winning the argument but about winning hearts, and when we connect before we correct, we can respond to hard questions without compromising God's grace or truth.

Book	Study Guide	DVD
9780718091538	9780310088578	9780310088592

Available now at your favorite bookstore,
or streaming video on StudyGateway.com.

Do you find yourself asking, "What do I do next? How do I stay motivated to grow deeper in my relationship with God when I feel complacent, intimidated, or confused? What can I do to get back on track when I hit a spiritual rut?" In *What's Next?*, bestselling author and pastor Chris Hodges offers a practical guide to all those looking for clarity and direction, and reveals the four steps to spiritual maturity.

In this five-session video Bible study and book Chris demonstrates how each step is part of both a linear path and a cycle leading to deeper levels of faith. No matter where you may be on the spiritual spectrum, *What's Next?* is the guide you need to find your next step, and discover the joy that comes walking the road of richer faith.

Book	Study Guide	DVD
9780718091569	9780310104124	9780310104148

Available now at your favorite bookstore,
or streaming video on StudyGateway.com.

Video Study for Your Church or Small Group

In this five-session video Bible study, bestselling author and pastor Chris Hodges draws on the story of Elijah to show no matter how powerful, accomplished, or successful we may be, we can all still succumb to fear, doubt, despair, and hopelessness. Like Elijah, we can become overcomers and press on to God-inspired victory.

Bible Study Guide + Streaming Video
9780310117513

DVD 9780310117537

Available now at your favorite bookstore,
or streaming video on StudyGateway.com.